Books in the Vision 2000 Program

The following books in the Vision 2000 Program are available or projected for future publication:

Vision 2000 (A Cycle)
Mission 2000 (B Cycle)
Action 2000 (C Cycle)
Challenge 2000
Bible 2000
Almanac 2000

Quantity discounts are available when ordering multiple copies. For further information on these books or discount offers, call or write:

Tabor Publishing
200 East Bethany Drive
Allen, Texas 75002–3804
Call toll free 800–822–6701

W9-BAX-112

BIBLE 2000

Genesis to Revelation— for Busy People

Mark Link, S.J.

TABOR®
PUBLISHING
Allen, Texas

IMPRIMI POTEST
Bradley M. Schaeffer, S.J.

NIHIL OBSTAT
Rev. Glenn D. Gardner, J.C.D.

IMPRIMATUR
† Most Rev. Charles V. Grahmann
Bishop of Dallas

October 25, 1994

The Nihil Obstat and Imprimatur are official declara-
tions that the material reviewed is free of doctrinal or
moral error. No implication is contained therein that
those granting the Nihil Obstat and Imprimatur agree
with the contents, opinions, or statements expressed.

ACKNOWLEDGMENT

Unless otherwise noted, Scripture quotations are from
Today's English Version text. Copyright © American
Bible Society 1966, 1971, 1976, 1992. Used by permission.

Send all inquiries to:
Tabor Publishing
200 East Bethany Drive
Allen, Texas 75002–3804

Printed in the United States of America

ISBN 0–7829–0459–9

1 2 3 4 5   98 97 96 95 94

CONTENTS

2 WORLD OF ABRAHAM

3 WORLD OF ISRAELITES

4 WORLD OF DAVID

5 WORLD OF PROPHETS

6 WORLD OF JESUS

8 WORLD OF PAUL

9 WORLD OF EARLY CHURCH

How to Use *Bible 2000*

There are two ways to use this book:

- on your own or
- as a member of a support group.

If you pray it on your own,
simply devote ten minutes a day
to each meditation exercise.

If you pray it as a member of a group,
you also meet with six to eight friends
once a week.

Guidelines for Meditating Daily

Begin each daily meditation by praying
the following prayer reverently:

Father, you created me
and put me on earth for a purpose.
Jesus, you died for me
and called me to complete your work.
Holy Spirit, you help me
to carry out the work
for which I was created and called.
In your presence and name—
Father, Son, and Spirit—
I begin my meditation.
May all my thoughts and inspirations
have their origin in you
and be directed to your glory.

The format for each meditation
is as follows:

- *Read* the meditation exercise slowly.
  When you finish, return to any
  phrase, sentence, or idea
  that struck you while reading.
  (Spend about one minute on this step.)

- *Think* about the phrase, sentence,
  or idea that struck you.
  Why did it strike you?
  (Spend about four minutes on this step.)

- *Speak* to God about your thoughts.
  Talk to God as you would to a close
  and trusted friend.
  (Spend about one minute on this step.)

- *Listen* to God's response.
  What may God wish to say to you?
  (Spend about four minutes on this step.)

End each meditation by reciting
the Lord's Prayer slowly and reverently.
Then jot down in a notepad
whatever struck you most
during your meditation.

N.B: The "Daily Meditation Format,"
including the opening meditation prayer,
is printed on the inside front cover
of *Bible 2000*.

Guidelines for Meeting Weekly

The purpose of the weekly meeting
is for *support* and *sharing*.
Meetings are 30 to 40 minutes long,
unless the group decides otherwise.
The meeting starts with a "Call to Prayer."
A member lights a candle and
the following prayer is said reverently:

FIRST READER
Jesus said,
"I am the light of the world. . . .
Whoever follows me
will have the light of life
and never walk in darkness."   JOHN 8:12

SECOND READER
Lord Jesus, you also said
that where two or three
come together in your name,
you are there with them.
The light of this candle
symbolizes your presence among us.

THIRD READER
And, Lord Jesus,
where you are, there, too,
are the Father and the Spirit.
And so we begin our meeting
in the presence and the name
of the Father,
the Son,
and the Holy Spirit.

The meeting proper begins with
the leader responding briefly
to these two questions.

1. How faithful was I to my commitment
   to reflect daily on the Bible reading?

2. Which daily meditation
   was most meaningful for me and why?

The leader then invites each member,
in turn, to respond briefly
to the same two questions.
When all have responded,
the leader opens the floor
to anyone who wishes

- to elaborate on his or her response
  to the second question or

- to comment on another's response
  (not to take issue with it,
  but to affirm or clarify it).

The meeting ends
with a "Call to Misson": a charge
to witness to Jesus and
to his teaching in daily life.
It consists
in praying the following reverently:

FIRST READER
We conclude our meeting
by listening to Jesus say to us

what he said to his disciples
in his Sermon on the Mount:

SECOND READER
"You are like light for the whole world.
A city built on a hill cannot be hid.
No one lights a lamp
and puts it under a bowl;
instead it is put on the lampstand,
where it gives light
for everyone in the house.
In the same way
your light must shine before people,
so that they will see the good things
you do and praise your Father in heaven."

MATTHEW 5:14–16

Then a member extinguishes the candle
(lit at the start of the meeting).

FINAL READER
The light of this candle
is now extinguished.
But the light of Christ in each of us
must continue to shine in our lives.
Toward this end
we pray together the Lord's Prayer:
"Our Father . . ."

For handy reference the "Call to Prayer"
and the "Call to Mission" are printed
on the inside back cover of this book.

1 World of Old Testament _____

Weeks
1   The Bible
2   Creation
3   De-creation

Timeline (key dates)

B.C.E. (Before Common Era)

C.E. (Common Era)

c. 3100 B.C.E.	Writing begins
c. 1200	Biblical writing begins
c. 250	Bible into Greek
c. 400 C.E.	Bible into Latin
c. 138	Bible into English
1947–56	Dead Sea Scrolls

Bible (key book)
Genesis (1:1–11:26)

MEDITERRANEAN
SEA

SEA OF
GALILEE

Jordan River

Qumran

DEAD
SEA

Rapunzel was a beautiful girl
who lived in a tower with a witch.
The witch told her she was ugly,
and Rapunzel believed her.

One day a handsome prince
saw Rapunzel at a tower window.
He was stunned by her beauty.
To make a long story short,
he rescued her and married her.

This story and others like it
were passed on *orally* for centuries.
One reason they weren't written down
is that most people then couldn't read.

Education and printing changed that.
Books became popular
and oral storytelling began to decline.
Eventually, only the elderly remembered
many of the older stories.
These stories would die when they died.

To keep this from happening,
two brothers in Germany, the Grimms,
had the elderly people recite the stories
so that they could record them.

The brothers eventually found, edited,
and recorded nearly a hundred stories.
Among them were "Snow White,"
"Cinderella," and "Sleeping Beauty."

A situation similar to the one in Germany
existed in ancient Israel.
For centuries, the people passed on
the story of God's dealings with them
almost exclusively by word of mouth.

Then scribes were inspired by God
to collect, edit, and record this history.
The result is the origin
of the written version of the Bible.

And so the Bible developed gradually
over a number of centuries,
by three stages:

- *Life*   the *actual event*
  of Israel leaving Egypt
- *Oral*   *retelling of the event*
  to current generation
- *Written*   *recording of the event*
  for new generations

Spiritual writers recommend
that I do for myself
what the scribes did for Israel:
keep a record of God's dealings with me
as I do this meditation program.
And so starting today, I will write down
some thought (a sentence or two)
that struck me during my meditation.

Most people today think of the Bible
as being one book.
Actually, it is a library of books
that is divided into two main parts:

- *Old Testament* (Hebrew Scriptures),
  written before Jesus' coming, and
- *New Testament* (Christian Scriptures),
  written after Jesus' coming.

The books of the Old Testament,
in turn, may be divided into four groups:

- Torah (Pentateuch)   5 books
- Historical   16 books
- Wisdom   7 books
- Prophetic   18 books

Surprisingly, some of our oldest copies
of biblical books were found in 1947
at Qumran, northwest of the Dead Sea.
They were written on scrolls,
now known as the "Dead Sea Scrolls."
Their discovery reads like a novel.

A young man was tending his goats.
When one of them disappeared,
he went up a hillside in search of it.
Coming upon a hole in the hillside,
he threw a stone through it.
When he heard something break,
he panicked and ran.

The next day he returned with his cousin.

Climbing through the hole . . . ,
they first groped in darkness. . . .
They made out some jars with lids. . . .
They opened one; it was empty. . . .
They opened still another
and from this one they took some hides
that were rolled up and inscribed.
ROLAND DE VAUX, "The Qumran Story," *The Bible Today Reader*

The boys' discovery touched off a hunt
for more scrolls hidden in caves.
It produced these remarkable results:

- Between 1947 and 1956,
  eleven caves yielded 800 documents
  (mostly in fragmentary form).
- Some 200 of these documents were
  biblical writings that contained
  every book of the Hebrew Bible
  except the Book of Esther.

Most scholars think that Essenes
(Jewish "monks") living at Qumran
hid the scrolls around 70 C.E.
to protect them from invading Romans.

What are some questions I have
about the Dead Sea Scrolls as I read
about their surprise discovery?

11

Scientists used four methods to date
the Dead Sea Scrolls:

- writing styles of the scrolls,
- coins found with the scrolls,
- pottery used to store the scrolls,
- carbon 14 dating.

Describing the latter method,
Popular Science magazine said:

Willard F. Libby,
University of Chicago radio chemist,
burned fragments of the linen wrappings
around the scrolls to pure carbon.
Then he measured their radioactivity.

Concerning the use of radioactive carbon,
Popular Science writes:

When the atom bomb first mushroomed
its message of death and destruction . . .
there were many who speculated
on the future uses of atomic energy. . . .
[Few] put Bible study on their list. . . .
[Now] the seeming miracle
has come to pass. . . . Cosmic rays that
bombarded the earth when Christ was
born have left behind a coded message
for nuclear physicists to decipher.

Three points may be made
about the importance of the scrolls.

First, they are a thousand years older
than the oldest Hebrew texts
known to us before this discovery.
For example, some of the scrolls go back
a hundred years before Jesus' birth.
At least one scroll
goes back three hundred years before it.

Second, the scrolls fill in Jewish history
between 300 B.C.E. and 70 C.E.,
where somewhat of a void has existed.

Third, the scrolls help to shed light
on some biblical events and people.
For example, John the Baptist
uses figures of speech (MATTHEW 3:7) and
follows religious practices (MATTHEW 11:18)
described in the scrolls.
This led scholar Otto Betz to say:

*It is reasonable to conclude
that John the Baptist was raised
in the tradition of the Essenes and
may well have lived at Qumran
before taking his message
to a wider public.*

*Some people think God may have
purposely let the scrolls stay hidden
until modern times. What do I think?*

13

Early scrolls were made of papyrus,
a paperlike product made from reeds
that grew along the Nile in Egypt.

Sheets the size of typing paper
were glued or sewed together
in lengths of about thirty feet.
Then they were rolled up.

Eventually, leather replaced papyrus.
Almost all the Dead Sea Scrolls
were made of leather.

Scribes wrote with reeds
whose point had been shredded
to form a tiny brush.
Moreover, they followed strict rules
when making a copy of a biblical scroll.

First, they meditated on this holy task.
Then they set before themselves
the scroll to be copied.
Commenting on it, Robert Aron says:

The scribe must refer to it continuously
and never write a word
from his own memory
or without first pronouncing it aloud.
Special care must be taken
in writing the divine names.
Before each of these
the scribe must pronounce the formula:

"I intend to write the Holy Name."
If he forgets one single time,
the scroll is unfit to be read in public.
It must be entirely rewritten.
                                    The Jewish Jesus

Scribes did not divide the Bible
into chapters and verses.
Scholars did this many centuries later.

The Bible often refers to scrolls.
One reference describes Jesus reading
from a scroll of the prophet Isaiah:

[Jesus] unrolled the scroll and
found the place where it is written:
"The Spirit of the Lord is upon me,
because he has chosen me to bring
the good news to the poor. . . ."

Jesus rolled up the scroll . . .
[and] said to [the people],
"This passage of scripture
has come true today,
as you heard it being read."
                            LUKE 4:16–18, 20–21

What are my thoughts
as I imagine myself listening to Jesus?
What may have been Jesus' thoughts
as he read this particular passage?

15

The novel *The Last Temptation of Christ*
portrays Matthew with an open notebook.
Jesus enters and Matthew
shows him the notebook, saying,
"Rabbi, here I recount your works."

After reading a few lines, Jesus asks,
"Who told you these things?"
Matthew replies, "The angel."
Jesus asks, "What angel?"
Matthew replies, "The one who comes
each night, as I take up my pen to write.
He dictates what I should write."

Christians have always believed
that the Bible is inspired—
even though they understand and express
this belief in different ways.

How should we understand *inspiration?*
We need to avoid two extremes.

First, we must not imagine
that the Holy Spirit or an angel
dictated the Bible word for word.
Second, we should not imagine that
the Holy Spirit's role
was only that of spiritual "watchdog"
keeping the human writers from error.

Rather, we should picture
the Holy Spirit and the human author

as both being actively involved.
And so we may describe inspiration
this way:

Inspiration means the Holy Spirit
worked *in* and *through* the human writers
in such a way that they were empowered
to use their own talents and words
to communicate what God
wanted them to communicate.

Because the Bible is inspired,
it is free from error
in matters that relate to salvation.

This does not mean
it is free, also, in matters
that relate to history and science.
God never intended to write books
on science and history.

Nor is the Bible free from such errors.
Deuteronomy 14:7 says
hares chew cud, which is incorrect.
1 Samuel 31:4 says Saul killed himself,
while 2 Samuel 1:9–10 says
that an Amalekite killed him.

How do I understand these words:
"The Bible is the word of God
expressed in the words of humans"?

A woman said, "A number of ancient
writings claim to be gospels.
(Gospel of Thomas, Gospel of James)
How do we know which are inspired?"

Christians believe the same Holy Spirit
who guided the human writers
in composing the Bible guided the Church
in discerning which books are "inspired."
This list of inspired books is called the
canon of the Bible.

Catholic and Protestant churches
agree on the New Testament canon,
but not on the Old Testament canon.
The reason goes back before Jesus' birth.

Between 300 B.C.E. and 150 B.C.E., the Old
Testament was translated into Greek,
because most Jews living outside
Palestine no longer spoke Hebrew.
The Greek translation
was called the *Septuagint* ("seventy"),
after the number of Jewish scholars
reportedly involved in the project.

Christians (most of whom spoke Greek)
adopted the Septuagint
as their "official" Old Testament text.
New Testament writers—
like Matthew, Mark, Luke, and John—
quoted from it over 300 times.

The Septuagint contained seven books—
and parts of two books—that modern
Jews omit from their official canon:

Judith	Sirach
Tobit	Baruch
1–2 Maccabees	Esther (long version)
Wisdom	Daniel (long version)

Ancient Jews living inside Palestine
gradually distanced themselves from
Greek-speaking Jews outside Palestine—
and from the Septuagint as well.

Decades after Jesus' ascension,
Palestinian Jews adopted a new canon,
omitting the books listed above.
Modern Jews and modern Protestants
follow the later Palestinian listing;
Catholics follow the Septuagint listing.

*A girl said, "Not all biblical books
are equal in importance. If we imagine
these books like concentric circles,
the gospels are at the center.
The lesser important books ripple out
from them. Christians should focus
on the inner circles that unite us,
not on the outer ripples that divide us."
How do I feel about her statement?*

19

A high school girl asked,
"Some call the word of God the Bible.
Others call it Scripture. Who is right?"

The answer is, "Both are right."
The word *Bible* comes from
a Greek word meaning "The Books."
The word *Scripture* comes from
a Latin word meaning "The Writings."

Some people also ask about the terms
Old Testament and *New Testament*.

- *Testament* comes from a Greek word
  meaning "covenant" or "sacred pact."
- *Old Testament* refers to
  God's covenant with Israel,
  mediated through Moses.
- *New Testament* refers to
  God's covenant with all people,
  mediated through Jesus.

Some Old Testament writings date from
about 1200 B.C.E. (Before the Common Era).
These writings—along with
oral traditions of the Bible—were later
collected and recorded on scrolls.

Between 300 B.C.E. and 150 B.C.E., the entire
Old Testament was translated into Greek.
One of the oldest Greek translations
of the entire Bible

is the fourth-century Codex Siniaticus.
(A *codex* is a manuscript in book form,
rather than in scroll form.)

Around 400 C.E., Saint Jerome
translated the Septuagint into Latin.
This translation became known
as the *Vulgate* ("common" version).
The first complete English translation
came in the fourteenth century.

The following are translations
of the same Old Testament passage.
The first version translates the words*;*
the second translates the thought*.*

1. *"[The day is coming when]*
   the grinders are idle
   because they are few, and . . .
   the doors to the street are shut,
   and the sound of the mill is low." (NAB)
2. *"[The day is coming when]*
   your teeth will be too few
   to chew your food. . . .
   Your ears will be deaf to the noise
   of the street. You will barely be able
   to hear the mill as it grinds." (TEV)

   ECCLESIASTES 12:3–4

Which version do I prefer and why?
What danger do I see in the second?

In March 1925, Tennessee passed a law
forbidding schools to teach any theory
that denies the biblical story of creation.

To test the constitutionality of the law,
the American Civil Liberties Union
arranged to have a biology teacher,
John Scopes, break the law.
Clarence Darrow, a prominent
criminal lawyer, agreed to defend him.

To offset Darrow's fame and prestige,
the prosecution enlisted the aid
of William Jennings Bryan,
a former presidential candidate.

On July 10, 1925, the courtroom
in Dayton, Tennessee, was jammed.

Darrow surprised everyone
by calling Bryan to the stand.
Then he read this biblical passage:
"Evening passed and morning came—
that was the first day."

He asked Bryan, "Do you believe
the sun was created on the fourth day—
as the Bible says later on?"
Bryan answered, "I do!"

Then Darrow asked him,
"Can you tell me how it is possible

to have morning and evening
on the first day if the sun
isn't created until the fourth day?"
Snickers rippled across the courtroom.

Next Darrow asked Bryan,
"Do you believe God punished the snake
by making it to crawl—as the Bible says?"
Bryan said, "I do!"

Then Darrow asked him, "Can you tell me
how snakes moved about before that?"
Laughter swept across the courtroom.

Bryan exploded! "Your honor,
this man, who doesn't believe in God,
is using this court to ridicule him."

Darrow shouted, "I object!
I'm simply questioning your fool ideas
that no thinking Christian believes."

How would I answer
Darrow's first question to Bryan:
"Can you tell me how it is possible
to have morning and evening
the first day
if the sun isn't created until
the fourth day?"
How do I explain apparent contradictions
in the Bible?

23

The Bible portrays God
creating the universe in six days:

In the beginning, when God created
the universe, the earth was formless . . .
[and] in total darkness. . . .

Then God commanded,
"Let there be light"—and light appeared.
God was pleased . . . [and] separated
the light from the darkness. . . .
[God] named the light "Day"
and the darkness "Night."
Evening passed and morning came—
that was the first day. . . .

Then God commanded,
"Let there be a dome . . . [to separate
the water above it from the water
below it]"—and it was done. . . .
[God] named the dome "Sky."
Evening passed and morning came—
that was the second day.

Then God commanded,
"Let the water . . . [be separated
from the land]"—and it was done.
[God] named the land "Earth," and the
water . . . "Sea." And God was pleased. . . .
Evening passed and morning came—
that was the third day.

Then God commanded,
"Let lights appear in the sky to separate
day from night. . . ." And God was pleased. . . .
Evening passed and morning came—
that was the fourth day. . . .

By the seventh day God [was done]. . . .
[God] blessed the seventh day
and set it apart as a special day. . . .
That is how the universe was created.
GENESIS 1:1–10, 13–14, 18–19; 2:2–4

The biblical author describes each day
of creation in a repetitive, poetic style:

- an introduction *God commanded,*
- a command *"Let there be light."*
- the execution *Light appeared.*
- the celebration *God was pleased.*
- the conclusion *Evening passed.*

This style is much like that found in
many children's books. The author uses
it because he is addressing people who,
like children, can't read or write.
The style is entertaining to listen to,
easy to remember, and simple to repeat.

What does the creation story's style
suggest concerning whether or not
I should interpret it literally? Why?

Bible readers cluster
into two main groups: *literalists*
(fundamentalists) and *contextualists*.

Literalists, like Bryan,
interpret the Bible literally, saying,
"It means exactly what it says!"

But not every literalist agrees
on how literally to interpret the Bible.
For example, Jehovah's Witnesses
say you *may* interpret the word *day*
as "era"—as in "Lincoln's day."

Church of God members say you *must*
interpret *day* to mean "24 hours."
Thus, following a literal "Bible calendar,"
they hold that creation took place
about 6,000 years ago.

People ask, "How can they believe this,
when science *proves* planet Earth
is millions of years old?"
Literalists reply, "Read your Bible!"

In the beginning,
when God created the universe,
the earth was formless and desolate.
The raging ocean that covered everything
was engulfed in total darkness. . . .
Then God commanded, "Let there be light."
GENESIS 1:1–3

Literalists say the word *then*
implies that planet Earth already existed
before God said, "Let there be light."
Therefore, the Bible is describing
the *preparation* of Earth for habitation,
not the actual *creation* of Earth.

Literalists answer Darrow's first question,
saying that the sun already existed,
but that something prevented its light
from reaching Earth. They add:

Venus [blanketed by ultra thick clouds]
illustrates what may have been the
condition of its neighbor planet Earth
up until the "fourth day."
WATCH TOWER BIBLE AND TRACT SOCIETY

Literalists have a bigger problem
trying to explain the presence
of two creation stories in the Bible.
The first (GENESIS 1:1–31) says
that God created people last;
the second (GENESIS 2:4b–25) contradicts it,
saying that God created people first.

Wasn't the biblical writer aware
of the obvious contradiction contained
in the two creation stories?
Why place them back-to-back anyway?

Contextual interpreters
hold that to determine the meaning
of a number of biblical passages,
we need to study both the *text*
and the *context* of the passage.
A modern example illustrates why.

Truck drivers often use "CB talk"
when communicating with
one another over their CB radios.
For example,
they use phrases like *motion lotion,*
seat covers, and *nap traps.*

In a CB-radio context,
these phrases have a different meaning
than the one they normally have.
For example,
motion lotion means "gas";
seat covers means "passengers";
nap traps means "motels."

What is true of CB communication
is also true of Bible communication.
A knowledge of its *context* is sometimes
essential to understanding its *text*.

Take the first creation story.
The historical and cultural context
in which it was composed
reveals four important facts
that help us understand the text itself.

First, most ancient peoples
could not read or write.
They learned mostly by word of mouth.

Second, most people of that time
believed in many gods (polytheism)
rather than one God (monotheism).

Third, people had different ideas
about how the world came about.
For example, some believed
it came about by accident, not by plan.
(Some people still believe this.)

Finally, people had different ideas
about created things.
For example, some people believed
the human body was created evil,
because it seemed to war against
our efforts to do what we should.

It is within this historical context that
we must interpret the creation story.

*How does the context of the creation
story shed light on these questions:*
- *Should we interpret it literally?*
- *Are there many gods?*
- *Did the world come about by chance?*
- *Was the human body created evil?*

The first teaching
of the creation story emerges
when we recall
that it was written at a time
when people worshiped all kinds of gods:
humans, animals, the moon, the sun
(DEUTERONOMY 4:16–19).

Within this context, the biblical writer
portrays God creating these things—
the very things
that people of that time worshiped.

The writer's point?
If God created these things,
how can they be "gods"?

And so the first teaching is this:
God is one, not many.

The second teaching becomes clear
when, again, we consider its context.
It was written at a time
when many people believed
the world came into being by chance.

Within this cultural context,
the Bible portrays God
creating the world according to a plan.
And so the second teaching is this:
God created everything;
creation didn't happen by chance.

The third teaching emerges when
we recall that the creation story was
written at a time when many people
believed the human body was evil.

Within this context,
the biblical writer portrays God
affirming the "goodness" of everything:
"God looked at everything he had made,
and he was very pleased" (GENESIS 1:31).
And so the third teaching is this:
God created everything good.

Finally, the creation story was written
at a time when all days
were considered to be the same.
Within this context, the biblical writer
portrays God blessing the seventh day.
And so the fourth teaching is this:
God created the Sabbath special.

And so the creation story teaches
four revolutionary, religious truths:

- God is one;
- God created everything;
- God created everything good;
- God created the Sabbath special.

If God created everything good,
where did evil come from?

31

In his poem "Creation"
James Weldon Johnson describes
the "Great God" kneeling down in the mud.
God labors and labors over a lump of clay
until, at last, it takes the shape
of God's own glorious image.

This delightful image of God
introduces the second creation story:

The LORD God took some soil . . .
formed a man out of it . . .
[and] breathed life-giving breath
into his nostrils. GENESIS 2:7

The second creation story raises
a question: Why two creation stories?

Recall that the Book of Genesis
was passed on orally for centuries.
There were, apparently,
two "creation stories" or traditions.
So when the sacred writer was inspired
to record them, he put them back-to-back.

The second creation story complements
the first in two ways.

First, it reveals the intimate union
creation set up between God and people.
It is a union that is even closer
than a mother to her child (ISAIAH 49:15).

Second, it reinforces the revelation
that God gave human beings a share
in the divine power and dominion
over the rest of creation (GENESIS 1:26).

It portrays God
bringing the birds and the animals
to the human beings to be named (GENESIS 2:19).

Naming something is a symbolic way
of showing that the person naming it
has power over it.

Thus the second story complements
the first story in two ways:

- It reveals the intimate union creation
  set up between God and humans.
- It reinforces the revelation that humans
  share in God's power and dominion
  over the rest of creation.

What are my thoughts
as I imagine God appearing right now
and saying to me lovingly,
"Can a woman forget her own baby
and not love the child she bore?
Even if a mother should forget her child,
I will never forget you." (ISAIAH 49:15)

The second creation story ends
with God creating the first woman.

NARRATOR   *Then the LORD God made*
              the man fall into a deep sleep,
              and while he was sleeping,
              he took out one of the man's
              ribs and closed up the flesh.
              He formed a woman out of the
              rib and brought her to him. . . .

MAN   *Here is one of my own kind—*
              Bone taken from my bone,
              and flesh from my flesh.
              "Woman" is her name because
              she was taken out of man.

NARRATOR   *That is why a man leaves*
              his father and mother
              and is united with his wife,
              and they become one.

                              GENESIS 2:21–24

Hebrew society, like most ancient ones,
was dominated by men.
Women were an oppressed minority.
They were valued, primarily,
as bearers of children—especially male:
warriors and workers.
Contextualists interpret the story
of God's creation of woman as a rejection
and a correction of that social structure.
It does this in a twofold way.

First, it repeats the teaching
of the first creation story,
which portrays God blessing humans—
male and female—with equal dignity.
They share the same

- image and likeness (GENESIS 1:27),
- power and dominion (GENESIS 1:26),
- flesh and bone (GENESIS 2:23).

Second, it portrays God calling them
to a union so intimate
that they "become one" (GENESIS 2:24).

The intimacy of this union is akin to that
between God and humans. They share
God's own "life-giving breath" (GENESIS 2:7).
As a result, they are as close to God
as they are to their own breath.

And so the second creation story teaches
two revolutionary truths:
God calls humans—male and female—

- to a dignity that is equal and
- to an intimacy that makes them one.

*"When marriage works, nothing on earth
can take its place."* HELEN GAHAGAN DOUGLAS
What am I doing to make it work?

35

Time writer Lance Morrow says
there should be a "Dark Willard."
This "sick" newscaster would stand
before TV cameras each morning
to recite the morning "evil report."

On the wall behind Willard
would be a big map with ugly blotches
to show the places where "evil" defeated
"good" that night: crime in America,
floods in India, race riots in Africa.

"Dark Willard" raises a question:
If God created everything good,
how did evil enter our world?

The Bible answers this question
with a series of stories.
We may call them "de-creation stories,"
stories of how evil defeats goodness.

The stories start with a snake tempting
Adam and Eve to eat something
that God forbids them to eat, saying:

[God] knows that when you eat it,
you will be like God and know
what is good and what is bad. . . .

As soon as they had eaten it,
they were given understanding and
realized that they were naked. GENESIS 3:5–7

Contextualists interpret this story
the way they do the creation story—
as a *symbolic* story.
The key to understanding it
is the symbolism of the word *eating*.

Recall that the snake told Adam and Eve
that if they ate from the tree,
they would "be like God and know
what is good and what is bad."
The symbolism is this: *to eat* is *to know*.

To eat is a symbolic way of saying
the first couple *learned* "evil"
by becoming evil. They "tasted" it.
They did something evil.
Since they were good and became evil,
they now *know* the difference
between good and evil.

And so evil enters the world
through the sin of the first couple.

James Farrell says in Studs Lonigan:
"I'd like to see God. . . .
I'd like to say, 'God, why did you
create men and make them . . .
live brief unhappy lives like pigs, and . . .
die disgustingly and rot?' "
If I were God, how might I answer Studs?

Archaeology shows
that ancient peoples used nakedness
as a symbol of defeat and disgrace.

For example, stone slabs
found while digging up ancient palaces
show soldiers being slain naked
or paraded naked before their victors.

The biblical writer borrows this symbol
and invests it with a spiritual meaning.
He uses it to dramatize Adam and Eve's
defeat and disgrace by the snake:

As soon as [the man and the woman]
had eaten [the fruit], they . . .
realized that they were naked . . .
and covered themselves. GENESIS 3:7

Earlier the biblical writer said,
"The man and the woman were both naked,
but . . . not embarrassed" (GENESIS 2:25).

Embarrassment *after* sin
(not there before it) symbolizes
that sin destroyed something inside them.
They feel uncomfortable and guilty.
They feel alienated from themselves.

Thomas Merton gives a modern example
of such an "alienating" experience
in his book *The Seven Storey Mountain.*

He describes how, after high school,
he began living a wayward life.

Then one night
the realization of what he was doing
hit him in a horrifying way. He writes:

*I was overwhelmed with a sudden
and profound insight into the misery
and corruption of my own soul.
I was filled with horror at what I saw,
and my whole being rose up in revolt
against what was within me, and
my soul desired escape . . . from all this
with an intensity and an urgency
unlike anything I had ever known.*

This is the kind of experience
Adam and Eve had after their sin.

And so the first effect of sin
is *alienation from self—*
a loss of inner peace and joy.

*"It is one thing to mourn sin
because it exposes us to hell . . .
and another thing to mourn it because
it is wrong and offensive to God.
It is one thing to be terrified,
another, to be humbled."* GARDINER SPRING
What is sin's usual effect on me?

39

The screenplay *The Seventh Seal*
contains a scene in which a knight
dialogues with Death about God.

KNIGHT   *Why should God hide . . .*
              in the mist . . . ?
              I want knowledge. . . .
              I want God to speak to me.
DEATH   *But God remains silent.*
KNIGHT   *I call out to God in the dark*
              but no one seems to be there.
DEATH   *Perhaps no one is there.*
                           (Slightly adapted)

This dialogue
leads us to the second effect of sin.
The Bible says:

The LORD God
called out to the man, "Where are you?"
He answered,
"I heard you in the garden;
I was afraid and hid from you,
because I was naked." . . .
God asked, "Did you eat the fruit . . . ?"
The man answered,
"The woman . . . gave me the fruit. . . ."
[The woman said,]
"The snake tricked me into eating it." GENESIS 3:9–13

Two important points
emerge from this dialogue.

First, it reaffirms the first effect
of sin: *alienation from self.*
It does this by portraying Adam and Eve
as being unable or unwilling
to accept responsibility for their sin.
Each passes the buck:
Adam to Eve, and Eve to the snake.

Second, the dialogue introduces us
to the second effect of sin:
alienation from God.
Adam and Eve are now uncomfortable
in God's presence.
They feel afraid of God.
They feel alienated and estranged.

And so the second effect of sin
is *alienation from God*—
estrangement from the loving God
who created them and shared
the divine image with them (GENESIS 1:27).

*"Sin has four characteristics:
self-sufficiency instead of faith,
self-will instead of submission,
self-seeking instead of benevolence,
self-righteousness instead of humility."*
E. PAUL HOVEY

*Which of these do I battle most?
Give an example to illustrate.*

41

[The LORD] said to the woman,
"I will increase . . .
your pain in giving birth. . . ."
[And the LORD] said to the man, . . .
"You will have to work hard and sweat
to make the soil produce . . .
until you go back to the soil from which
you were formed." GENESIS 3:16–17, 19

This introduces us to the third effect
of sin: *alienation from nature.*
The biblical writer portrays sin
as causing a loss of harmony between
the first couple and the rest of nature.

Even their own bodies rebel,
bringing down on them
suffering and death (physical evil).
Thus *physical* evil
is portrayed as entering the world
through sin (*moral* evil).

The first "de-creation" story ends
with God expelling the couple from
the garden and blocking their access
to the "tree of life" with a "cherubim"
(GENESIS 3:24, NRSV).

Archaeologists have shed light
on the tree of life and the cherubim.
The *tree of life* is a mythical *plant,*
thought to confer immortality

(freedom from death)
on those who have access to it.
We might compare it
to the fountain of youth that explorers
hoped to find in the "new world."

The *cherubim* is a mythical *beast*
with wings and a human head.
It was placed at entrances to buildings
to function as a kind of watchdog
to keep out unworthy intruders.

When we link these two symbols—
tree of life and *cherubim*—
we get the biblical writer's point.
Sin destroys the first couple's harmony
with the rest of nature.
They lose access to immortality
and become vulnerable to suffering and death.

Sin (moral evil) opens the door
to suffering and death (physical evil).
And so the third effect of sin
is *alienation from nature*.

*"[God's plan] is to bring all creation
together, everything in heaven and
on earth, with Christ as head"* (EPHESIANS 1:10).
*How do I see Paul's words
related to the third effect of sin?*

43

Marvin Gaye was a headline vocalist.
His career began at age seven,
when he began singing gospel songs
in his father's church in Washington, D.C.

Unfortunately, a deep hostility set in
between father and son.
As Marvin grew, so did the hostility.
On April 1, 1984, it exploded into violence.
Marvin's father shot his son.

Gaye's biographer said of Marvin:

*He really believed in Jesus a lot,
but he could not apply
the teaching of Jesus on forgiveness
to his own father.
In the end it destroyed them both.*
DAVID RITZ, *Divided Soul*

The Marvin Gaye story is a tragic echo
of the biblical story of Cain and Abel.
As these two family members grew,
so did Cain's jealousy of Abel.
Then one day it exploded into violence.

CAIN   *Let's go out in the fields.*
NARRATOR   *When they were
            out in the fields,
            Cain turned on his brother
            and killed him.*
LORD   *Where is your brother Abel?*

CAIN	*I don't know. Am I supposed to take care of my brother? . . .*
LORD	*Your brother's blood is crying out to me. . . .*
NARRATOR	*Cain went away from the LORD's presence.*

GENESIS 4:8–10, 16

The Cain and Abel story
brings us to the fourth effect of sin:
alienation from other people.
Sin estranges us from one another—
even from members of our own family.
Instead of living with them harmoniously,
as God intended, we do just the opposite.

And so the effects of sin
continue to multiply in a tragic way.
Sin alienates us from

- self   (awareness of nakedness),
- God   (hiding from God),
- nature   (pain and death), and
- others   (Cain's slaying of his brother).

*"Sins are like circles in the water
when a stone is thrown into it;
one produces another.
When anger was in Cain's heart,
murder was not far off."* PHILIP HENRY
What are some sin-circles in my life?

45

The TV series *Roots* played
to a record 130 million viewers.
Based on a Pulitzer-prize-winning book,
it dramatized Alex Haley's search for
his African ancestry ("family tree").
It also sent viewers in droves to libraries
to research their own family trees.

Genesis lists two family trees.
The first starts with Adam
and ends with Noah (GENESIS 5:1–32).
The second starts with Noah's son and
ends with Abraham (GENESIS 11:10–26).
Their purpose is symbolic and twofold.
They allow the biblical writer

• to move rapidly through history
  from Adam (father of all people)
  to Abraham (father of Hebrew people) and
• to show rapidly the increase in sin:
  Adam dies at the age of 930;
  Abraham's father, at the age of 205.

This decline in life spans symbolizes
a dramatic increase in sin:
Sin brings sickness and death;
sickness and death shorten life spans.
The result is tragic.

NARRATOR   *God looked at the world*
            and saw that it was evil. . . .

GOD	*[to Noah] I have decided to*
	put an end to all people. . . .
	Build a boat [ark]. . . .
	Go into the boat
	with your whole family. . . .
NARRATOR	*Rain fell on the earth*
	forty days and nights. . . .
	It covered the highest mountains.

GENESIS 6:12–14; 7:1, 12, 19

Literalists interpret this story as fact.
That is why they sponsor expeditions
to locate Noah's ark, which the Bible
says came to rest after the flood
on the mountains of Ararat (GENESIS 8:4).

Contextualists interpret the story
as being symbolic.
Some feel it is totally symbolic.
Most think it is factual-symbolic.
It is *factual* in that the biblical writer
bases the story on a flood tradition.
It is *symbolic* in that the writer
uses the tradition to communicate
an important religious truth:
Sin leads to the destruction
of ourselves and our world.

*Why are literalists so eager
to find the remains of Noah's ark?*

The "de-creation" stories end
with the Tower of Babel story.
It takes place after Noah's descendants
repopulate the earth.
The people say:

*"Let's build a city with a tower
that reaches the sky, so that we can
make a name for ourselves."*   GENESIS 11:4

God confuses their speech,
their project fails, and they are scattered
"all over the earth" (GENESIS 11:9).

Archaeology has shed light on this story.
The *ziggurat* (meaning "mountain peak")
was intended as a meeting place
for gods and people.

Some people think the purpose
of the Tower of Babel story is to explain
the origin of nations and languages.
But within the *context*
of the series of "de-creation" stories,
the biblical writer
has a deeper purpose in mind.

The writer uses the story
to introduce us to the fifth effect of sin:
alienation of people (groups or nations)
from other people.
Sin is the root of prejudices and wars.

And so sin alienates us
not only from self, God, nature,
and other people (individuals),
but also from other groups of people
(nations and races).

When we finish reading
the "de-creation" stories (GENESIS 3–11),
we get this bleak impression:
People, individually and collectively,
are trapped in a giant whirlpool of sin.
Every person is doomed to be caught
in its all-engulfing destructive power.

This tragic "state" or situation
is sometimes called
the state of *original sin*.
We may sum it up in this threefold way:
The first sin of the first couple

- opens the door to evil in the world,
- flaws the human race, and
- dooms all to destruction.

Given *people* as they are (sin-prone),
and given the *world* as it is (sin-filled),
neither can survive
unless God intervenes to save them.

*What are some ways that I feel
the effects of original sin in my life?*

49

2 World of Abraham

Weeks

4   Re-creation
5   Preparation

Bible (key books)

Genesis (11:26–25:18)
Exodus (1:1–12:36)

Mark Twain wrote a story
about a group of people who get trapped
in a hopeless situation.
It is like having them on a plane
ten feet away from crashing into a cliff.

Twain doesn't want these people to die,
but he doesn't know how to save them.
So he ends his story, saying,
"I can't save these people;
if you think you can,
you are welcome to try."

Thousands of years ago
the world was in a hopeless situation.
Sin was destroying everything.
But God had a plan to save the world,
and that's what the Bible is all about.

We may think of the Bible as taking
the form of a stage play in three acts.

Act 1: *creation*   (God creates us),
Act 2: *de-creation* (sin destroys us),
Act 3: *re-creation* (God saves us).

That leads us to the Book of Genesis.
It has fifty chapters:
The first two chapters treat creation,
the next nine treat de-creation, and
the last thirty-nine treat re-creation.
Chapters 1–11 (creation and de-creation)

treat *prehistory times* (era of no records).
They are narrated in *symbol* stories.
Chapters 12–50 (re-creation) treat
folk-history times (era of oral records).
They are narrated in *folk stories*,
stories passed on orally for centuries.

Chapter 12 opens in Haran,
where Abram had migrated from Ur.
From this city God called Abram, saying:

*"Leave your country . . .
and go to a land [Canaan]
that I am going to show you."* GENESIS 12:1

This important event
is often referred to as Abram's "call."
It begins a pattern that repeats itself
over and over in biblical history.
Certain people experience an "inner call"
to leave all and embark upon a mission
that God reveals to them only gradually.

Abram is the first
in this long line of illustrious people.

*How does a knowledge of the era
in which a biblical event takes place
(prehistory or folk history)
give me a clue as to how literally
I should interpret it?*

Abram eventually reached Canaan.
The future lay ahead, shrouded in mystery.
All he could do was wait for further
revelation from God. One night it came:

GOD   *Do not be afraid, Abram. . . .*
             Look at the sky
             and try to count the stars;
             you will have
             as many descendants. . . .
             Bring me a cow, a goat,
             and a ram. . . .

NARRATOR   *Abram brought the animals . . .*
             cut them in half
             and placed the halves
             opposite each other. . . .
             When the sun
             was going down, Abram
             fell into a deep sleep. . . .
             A flaming torch suddenly
             appeared and passed
             between the pieces. . . .
             The LORD made a covenant
             with Abram.

GOD   *I promise to give your*
             descendants all this land.

                        GENESIS 15:1, 5, 9–10, 12, 17–18

This unusual ritual
is called "cutting a covenant."
Unlike modern nations and peoples,

ancients "cut a covenant,"
rather than "sign a treaty" or contract.

The contracting parties walked between
the halves of a divided animal.
The meaning of this unusual ritual
is preserved in the Bible:

[They] made a covenant with me
by walking between the two halves
of a bull. . . . So I will do to these people
what they did to the bull. JEREMIAH 34:18–19

Passing between the halves
signified that the two parties
would rather die a death
as violent as the death of the animals
than break the covenant they had "cut."

Abram's second encounter with God
puts into clearer focus
the reason why God had called him:
He is to father a nation that will enjoy
a unique relationship with God.

What are my thoughts
as I imagine myself to be Abram,
leaving my familiar surroundings
and embarking on a mysterious journey
with no idea where God is leading me
and what God has in store for me?

In Abram's time,
Canaan (modern Israel)
was under Egyptian control.

A portrait of daily life at that time
is preserved not only in Scripture
but also in Egyptian documents.
One such record is the "Story of Sinhue."

It concerns a man who is traveling
from Egypt to Canaan.
He runs out of water and his throat
is dry with the "taste of death."
At the last minute he is found and
saved by a Bedouin chief.

The "Story of Sinhue" goes on
to confirm existing biblical details
about daily life in Canaan.
Sinhue says:

It was a good land. . . .
Figs grew and so did grapes.
Wine was more available than water.
We had plenty of honey and olives.
There was every kind of fruit tree.

It is this land that the LORD promises
to Abram and his descendants.

As the years pass, however,
Sarai and Abram are still childless.
Then one day Sarai approaches Abram:

SARAI	*The LORD has kept me*
	from having children.
	Why don't you sleep with
	my slave? Perhaps
	she can have a child for me.
NARRATOR	*Hagar [the slave girl]*
	bore Abram a son,
	and he named him Ishmael.

GENESIS 16:2, 15

Archaeologists have helped to clarify
Sarai's unusual behavior. They unearthed
a library of clay tablets at Nuzi (in Iraq).
One tablet is a marriage contract
dating from Abraham's time.
It states that a sterile wife
has to provide her husband
with a substitute wife for childbearing,
so that his name, bloodline, and property
can be continued.

The Sinhue story and the Nuzi tablets
are two examples of how archaeology
is helping to shed light on the Bible.

What are my thoughts when I imagine
myself to be Abram, without offspring
after years of waiting? What might God
be saying to me by this situation?
How might it apply to my life today?

Ishmael's birth made Abram happy.
It paved the way for the fulfillment
of God's promise to him.
Then came an enormous surprise!
God spoke to Abram again:

"I am the Almighty God. . . .
Your name will no longer be Abram,
but Abraham. . . .
You and your descendants must all agree
to circumcise every male among you . . .
to show that my covenant with you
is everlasting. . . .

"You must no longer call
your wife Sarai; . . .
her name is Sarah. I will bless her,
and I will give you a son by her. . . .
You will name him Isaac."

GENESIS 17:1, 5, 10, 13, 15–16, 19

This third encounter with God
results in a new name and a mark
for the father of God's new people.

In the Bible, a new *name* for a person
is generally the sign of a new vocation.
Abraham's new name fits his new calling.
Abram means "exalted Father."
Abraham means "father of many."
Sarai's new name, *Sarah,* means
"princess" and fits her new vocation.

Abraham's *mark* is a sign of God's
covenant with him and his descendants.
It identifies them as belonging to
a privileged group: God's Chosen People.

*[And so Sarah] became pregnant
and bore a son to Abraham. . . .
Abraham named him Isaac,
and when Isaac was eight days old,
Abraham circumcised him.* GENESIS 21:2–4

After Isaac's birth, hostility erupts
between Sarah and Hagar.
Sarah prevails upon Abraham
to dismiss Hagar and Ishmael. God says:

*"I will also give many children
to the son of the slave woman,
so that they will become a nation.
He too is your son."* GENESIS 21:13

To this day, Arab nations trace
their ancestry back to Abraham
through his son Ishmael.
Abraham is also their faith-father.

*How significant is the fact
that Arabs, Jews, and Christians
share the same "faith-father"?
What might it be saying to us today?*

59

Human sacrifice
was not unusual in Abraham's time.
Novelist James Michener
discusses the ancient practice
in *The Source*.
He describes how the people of Makor
adopted a new god named Melak,
who demanded human sacrifice.

*[They adopted Melak] partly because
his demands upon them were severe,
as if this proved his power,
and partly because they had grown
somewhat contemptuous
of their local gods precisely because
they were not demanding enough.*

It is within this cultural context
that we should read the following:

NARRATOR   *Some time later,*
              God tested Abraham. . . .
GOD   *Take . . . your only son, Isaac,*
              whom you love so much,
              and go to the land of Moriah.
              There on a mountain . . . ,
              offer him as a sacrifice to me.
                              GENESIS 22:1–2

Abraham is confused and pained
by God's command, but he obeys.

NARRATOR	*Abraham cut some wood. . . .*
	Abraham made Isaac carry
	the wood for the sacrifice, and
	he himself carried a knife. . . .
	When they came to the place . . . ,
	Abraham built an altar. . . .
	He tied up his son and
	placed him on the altar. . . .
	Then he picked up the knife
	to kill him. . . .
ANGEL	*Abraham, Abraham! . . .*
	Don't hurt the boy. . . .
	Now I know that you
	honor and obey God,
	because you have not kept back
	your only son from him.

GENESIS 22:3, 6, 9–12

New Testament writers explain
Abraham's trial by fire this way:

It was faith that made Abraham
offer his son Isaac as a sacrifice
when God put Abraham to the test.

HEBREWS 11:17

Some people see Isaac as a "figure" of Jesus.
What obvious—and less obvious—
similarities do I see?

61

God's test of Abraham
highlights three points about faith.
It involves

- loving trust in God,
- constant struggle, and
- times of darkness.

First, it involves *loving trust* in God.
Abraham's heart rebels at the thought
of killing the son whom he loves deeply.
His mind also rebels.
Is not Isaac the one through whom
he will have descendants?

Second, faith involves *constant struggle*.
Just when Abraham thinks his faith
is solid, it is shaken
to the foundations by God's command.
Abraham discovers an important thing:
There is no such thing
as "getting the faith" and never again
having any difficulties.

Third, faith involves *times of darkness*.
Faith is like the sun.
Sometimes it shines brightly in the sky.
Sometimes it vanishes behind a cloud—
even seems to disappear entirely.
The agony such a faith "blackout"
can cause is strikingly illustrated
in *The Devil's Advocate* by Morris West.

One of its characters says
of God's "disappearance":

I groped for God and could not find God.
I prayed to God unknown
and God did not answer.
I wept at night for the loss of God. . . .
Then, one day, God was there again. . . .
I had never understood till this moment
the meaning of the words "gift of faith."

(Slightly adapted)

When faith seems to "black out"
and God becomes silent,
it helps to recall the following words.
They were found after World War II
on the cellar wall of a bombed-out house
in Cologne, Germany.

I believe in the sun
even when it is not shining.
I believe in love
even when I feel it not.
I believe in God
even when he is silent.

How do I resolve faith problems?
What advice might I give to a person
experiencing severe faith problems?
What are some faith problems I've had?
How did I solve them?

63

Egypt's President Anwar Sadat
did something on November 27, 1977,
that no previous Arab leader dared to do.
He risked the friendship of many Arabs
by going to Israel and addressing
the Knesset, the Israeli parliament.

In his address, Sadat noted the day was
Id al-Adha, an Islamic holy day that
celebrated Abraham's readiness
to sacrifice his son Isaac.

That day inspired
a similar "readiness" on his part to risk all
for peace between Arabs and Jews.

Sadat's words surprised many Christians.
They didn't realize that Muslims,
like Jews and Christians,
have Abraham as their faith-father.

Muslims trace their lineage through
Ishmael and Hagar; Jews and Christians,
though Isaac and Sarah.

Consider yet another modern example
of living out the faith we profess.
An inmate in a Chicago prison writes:

The past few months
I was confronted with the possibility
of legally losing any custody rights

*I may still possess to the dear son that
God entrusted to my late wife and me.*

Then he adds the "faith" dimension:

*I have been drawn several steps closer
to the experience of both Abraham
and our loving Creator—
who had especially strong attachments
to their sons.*

The prisoner ends, saying
that the story of Abraham and Isaac
helped him come to view his situation
as an opportunity
to grow in his faith and trust in God,
rather than view it as a catastrophe
to destroy his faith and trust.

*"It's not dying for faith that's so hard,
it's living up to it."*
WILLIAM MAKEPEACE THACKERAY
*The stories of Abraham and of Sadat,
and the story of the Chicago prisoner,
invite me to inventory my own readiness
to live my faith
more courageously and more faithfully.
What is one way I might—
with a little more effort—
live my faith better?*

A tourist in Iran was watching students
learning to weave rugs.
After a while, she asked a student,
"What happens if you make a mistake?"
The student said, "Our teacher doesn't
remove it, but finds a way to weave it
into the *overall* pattern of the rug."

God does something similar with people.
Take the case of Isaac.

Isaac marries Rebecca,
and they have two sons: Esau and Jacob.
One day Esau foolishly trades his firstborn
birthright (double inheritance) to Jacob
(DEUTERONOMY 21:17).

Years pass and Isaac grows old and blind.
He realizes it's time to bless Esau and
pass on to him his firstborn birthright.
Ignorant of Esau's trade with Jacob,
Isaac tells Esau to kill an animal and
prepare the special meal for doing this.

Jacob overhears the conversation.
When Esau departs,
Jacob prepares the proper meal hurriedly,
poses as Esau, and steals the blessing.
This story illustrates two points.

First, it illustrates
how God dealt with biblical people.

God did not program them to be saints
nor treat them like puppets.
God gave them the same free will
that God gives us.

When they acted foolishly or sinned,
God simply "wove" the new situation,
created by foolishness or sin,
into the pattern of salvation.

Second, it illustrates the Jewish belief
in the power of the spoken word
when uttered in important situations.
Once uttered, it cannot be revoked.
It is like an arrow shot from a bow;
it cannot be "unshot."

This explains why Isaac cannot revoke
the blessing when he learns what
Jacob has done (GENESIS 27:30–41).

When Esau discovers what has happened,
he plots to kill Jacob, but Jacob flees.

*"Sometimes we suffer
because God loves us enough
to give us the freedom to make mistakes."*
JOHN WIMMER
*How firmly do I believe that God also
loves me enough to give me the grace to
use mistakes to become a better person?*

Jacob flees and heads for Haran.
One night he comes upon a holy place
and decides to pitch camp there.
He builds a fire and falls asleep.

NARRATOR   *Jacob dreamed that he saw*
a stairway reaching from earth
to heaven, with angels going up
and coming down on it.
And there was the LORD
standing beside him.

GOD   *I am the LORD, the God*
of Abraham and Isaac. . . .
I will give to you
and to your descendants
this land . . . and through you
and your descendants
I will bless all the nations.

GENESIS 28:11–14

Jacob settles in Haran.
Later he returns to the dream site.
Again, he experiences God's presence.

GOD   *Your name is Jacob, but from*
now on it will be Israel. . . .

NARRATOR   *Then God left him. . . .*
Jacob named the place Bethel.

GENESIS 35: 10, 15

The stories of Abraham, Isaac, and
Jacob take the form of folk history.

68

Unlike scientific history,
it preserves the past in colorful stories
that can be easily remembered.

Folk history is real history.
It preserves tribal traditions.
For example, a Hebrew child might ask,
"Why are we called Israelites?" or
"Why do we pilgrimage to Bethel?"

And so, just as biblical *prehistory*
deals with such things
as the origin of the world and evil,
biblical *folk history*
deals with such things as the origin
of tribal traditions and customs.

In time, Israel (Jacob) returns to Canaan,
where he has twelve sons (Israelites),
forerunners of the twelve tribes.
He loves his son Joseph best of all,
because he is the son of his old age.

This makes Joseph's brothers so jealous
that they conspire to sell him as a slave
to traders, who take him to Egypt.

*"Jealousy is the tribute mediocrity pays
to genius."* FULTON SHEEN
*How do I handle my jealous feelings?
The jealous actions of others to me?*

69

The pyramids were a thousand years old
when Joseph walked into Egypt.
He must have stared wide-eyed at them.
He must have also stared wide-eyed
at the "sacred writings" (hieroglyphics)
that adorned Egyptian temples and tombs.

The slave traders
sold Joseph to an officer of the king.
The officer's wife was attracted to him.
When he ignored her, she accused him
falsely, and he was thrown into prison.
There he won fame interpreting dreams.
When the king heard of Joseph's ability,
he asked him to interpret two dreams.
Joseph obliged, saying:

*"The two dreams mean the same thing. . . .
There will be seven years of great plenty. . . .
After that . . . seven years of famine."*
GENESIS 41:25, 29–30

The king puts Joseph in charge of storing
grain during the "years of great plenty."
When the famine hits, Joseph's brothers
come to Egypt for grain.
After testing them to see if they've changed,
Joseph reveals himself to them.
He tells them to bring his father and
all their relatives to Egypt.
They settle in Goshen and prosper.

Archaeology supports
several details of the Joseph story.
For example, in Joseph's time
Egypt was overrun by Hyksos invaders.
This explains his rapid rise to power.
He did so in a time of political upheaval.

Records also show dream interpretation
was a highly respected art at that time.
Joseph had a very marketable talent.

Lastly, records tell of prolonged famines.
One preserves this lament of an official:

My heart is heavy over the failure
of the Nile floods for the past seven years . . .
there is a shortage of food in general.

The stories of the so-called patriarchs—
Abraham, Isaac, and Joseph—reveal
that God often chooses ordinary people,
even sinners, to play extraordinary roles
in the master plan of re-creation.
God doesn't ignore or erase their defects,
but weaves them into the overall plan.

Joseph told his brothers, "[Don't] blame
yourselves because you sold me here.
It was really God who sent me ahead
of you to save people's lives." GENESIS 45:5
What might I say to God about this mystery?

The Book of Genesis ends abruptly
with Joseph's death.
It is followed by the Book of Exodus
and a reversal of Hebrew fortune.
A new Egyptian king comes to power.
Gradually he oppresses the Israelites
by forcing them into slave labor.

*The Israelites
built the cities of Pithom and Rameses
to serve as supply centers for the king.*
EXODUS 1:11

The new king also orders the death
of all males born to Hebrew women.
It is during this period of oppression
that Moses is born.

Moses is saved from death
by the ingenuity of his mother.
She puts him in a watertight basket and
hides him in reeds at the river's edge.

Pharaoh's daughter finds the basket
while she is bathing in the river.
She realizes the child must be Hebrew,
but she prevails upon her father
to let her raise him as her son.

The story bears a similarity to
the legendary birth of Sargon of Akkad,
who lived years before Moses.

The Greek historian Herodotus reports
similar near-eastern "birth legends."
A narrow escape from death at birth
is a folk-history device
to show that the "blessing of the gods"
is upon the child.

Some scholars suggest
that Moses' marvelous escape
falls into such a folk-story category.
It points to the divine mission
he is destined to carry out.

In any event, when Moses grows up,
he grows aware of his Hebrew origins.
One day he sees an Egyptian foreman
beating a Hebrew slave.
He becomes angry, attacks the Egyptian,
and kills him.

Even though Moses
enjoys the favor of Pharaoh's family,
killing an Egyptian is
an unpardonable crime for a Hebrew.
Fearing for his life, he flees to Midian.
There he becomes a shepherd.

As I imagine myself to be Moses,
what are my thoughts
when I learn about my origins—
especially the stories of my birth?

One day Moses was tending his sheep.
He noticed a nearby bush on fire.
This wasn't so unusual.
Occasionally a bush caught fire in the
Sinai sun, but this bush didn't burn up.
Moses went over to see why.

GOD   *Do not come any closer.*
Take off your sandals,
because you are standing on
holy ground. I am the God of
your ancestors, the God of
Abraham, Isaac, and Jacob. . . .
I am sending you
to the king of Egypt so that
you can lead my people
out of his country.

MOSES   *I am nobody. How can I go*
to the king and bring
the Israelites out of Egypt?

GOD   *I will be with you. . . .*

MOSES   *When I go to the Israelites*
and say to them,
"The God of your ancestors
sent me to you," they will
ask me, "What is his name?"
So what can I tell them?

GOD   *I am who I am.*
You must tell them:
"The one who is called I AM

has sent me to you.". . .
This is my name forever.
EXODUS 3:5–6, 10–15

The expression "I am who I am"
brings us to the personal name for God.
Spelled YHWH (Hebrew has no vowels),
we translate it "LORD."

The meaning of YHWH is unknown.
Some speculate that "I am who I am"
might mean "I cannot be named or defined."

At one point in history, Jews ceased
to pronounce God's name out of fear.
In its place, they said *Adonai* ("Lord").
Thus the true pronunciation got lost.

Medieval scholars thought YHWH should
be pronounced *YaHoWaH*, or *Jehovah*.
Modern scholars say YHWH should be
pronounced *YaHWeH*, or *Yahweh*.

The significant thing is not
how God originally pronounced it,
but that God revealed it to Moses.
To tell another your name was to enter
into a trusting friendship with them.

As I imagine I am present when Jesus
says, "I Am Who I Am" (JOHN 8:24–59),
what are my thoughts?

75

Moses returned to Egypt a changed man.
He assumed leadership of the Israelites
and confronted Pharaoh.

MOSES   *The LORD, the God of Israel,*
            says, "Let my people go. . . ."

PHARAOH   *Who is the LORD?*
            Why should I listen to him
            and let Israel go?
            I do not know the LORD;
            and I will not let Israel go.
                                EXODUS 5:1–2

Nine times Moses confronts Pharaoh.
Nine times Pharaoh shouts, "No!"
Each refusal gives rise to a "plague":
the Nile turns to "blood"; frogs litter the land;
gnats swarm like dust;
boils infect and kill animals.

Commenting on the plagues,
Everyday Life in Bible Times
(National Geographic Society)
notes they may have been purely natural:

Silt and microbes redden the Nile
in flood. . . . Floodlands breed gnats
and mosquitoes. . . . Frogs breed. . . .
As frog swarms die,
vermin breed on the carcasses.
Pests such as the screwworm fly
inflame skin of man and beast.

Regardless of the origin of the plagues,
Pharaoh remains obstinate.
Then God tells Moses to prepare
for the final plague: the death of every
firstborn male in Egypt (EXODUS 12:12).

God instructs the Israelites
to sacrifice a lamb and smear its blood
on the outer door frame of their houses.
This will be a sign for the "angel of death"
to "pass over" that house (EXODUS 12:23).

Finally, God instructs the Israelites
to eat the lamb whose blood
has just saved them (EXODUS 12:26).
This joyful celebration becomes known
as the *Passover* and is still celebrated.

The final plague strikes in the middle
of the night (EXODUS 12:29–30).
Without even waiting for the sun to rise,
Pharaoh summons Moses and shouts,
"Get out, you and your Israelites! . . .
Take your sheep, goats, and cattle,
and leave" (EXODUS 12:31–32).
Moses leads the Israelites out of Egypt.

As I imagine I am a freed Israelite,
what are my thoughts as my family
and I follow Moses out of Egypt?

The Israelites had barely departed
when Pharaoh regretted freeing them.
He ordered his army to pursue them.
When the Israelites became aware
of this, they were terrified.
But at the LORD's command,

Moses held out his hand over the sea,
and the LORD drove the sea back
with a strong east wind.
It blew all night
and turned the sea into dry land.
The water was divided,
and the Israelites
went through the sea on dry ground,
with walls of water on both sides.

The Egyptians pursued them. . . .
The LORD . . . made the wheels
of their chariots get stuck, so that
they moved with great difficulty. . . .

The LORD said to Moses,
"Hold out your hand over the sea. . . ."
So Moses held out his hand over the sea,
and at daybreak the water returned
to its normal level . . .
and covered the chariots, the drivers,
and all the Egyptian army. . . .
On that day
the LORD saved the people of Israel . . .

*and they had faith in the LORD and
in his servant Moses.* EXODUS 14:21–28, 30–31

The Bible calls the place
where the people crossed *yam suph*.
Usually translated "Red Sea,"
it can also be translated "Reed Sea."
This latter translation suggests
that the place was marshlike,
typical of lake regions.

The Bible seems to support this
when it says of the Egyptians,
"The LORD . . . made the wheels
of their chariots get stuck."

Whether the "walls of water"
were an actual tidelike phenomenon
or a poetic flourish is debated.

There is no debate, however,
that the important point is not
what happened, but *why* it happened.
It is an affirmation of Israel's faith
that it was Yahweh
who delivered them from Egypt.

*As I imagine I am an Egyptian soldier,
what are my thoughts
as I return home and ponder the events
that have just taken place?*

79

3 World
of Israelites

Week

6   Covenant

Timeline (key dates—B.C.E)

c. 1290	Exodus
c. 1280	Covenant
c. 1250	Death of Moses

Bible (key books)

Genesis (25:19–55:26)
Exodus (12:37–40:38)

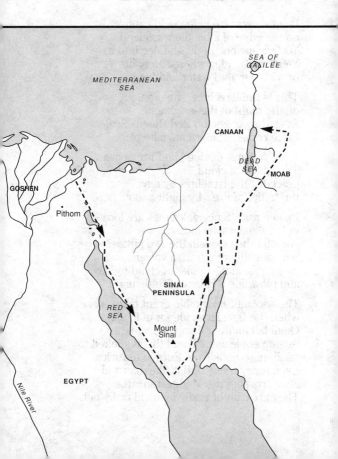

SEA OF GALILEE

MEDITERRANEAN SEA

CANAAN

DEAD SEA

MOAB

GOSHEN

Pithom

RED SEA

SINAI PENINSULA

Mount Sinai

EGYPT

Nile River

Imagine you are being held captive
on the edge of a hostile wasteland.
You escape one night and flee into it.
You have no idea where safety lies
or where to find water and food.

This is the Israelites' situation
on the night of the last plague.
After they cross the Red (Reed) Sea,
three remarkable events take place

First, "piliars" of cloud and fire appear.
The "pillar of cloud"
precedes the Israelites by day;
the "pillar of fire," by night (EXODUS 13:22).

People ask, "Since volcanoes are located
in the Sinai wasteland,
couldn't they explain the two pillars?
Smoke coiling up from a volcano
might resemble a pillar of cloud by day
and glow like a pillar of fire by night."

The second remarkable event takes place
when the Israelites run out of food:
Quail fall on their camp (EXODUS 16:13).
Again people ask, "Could this be linked to
quail migrations from Europe to Africa?"
Even today these birds fall exhausted
after crossing the Mediterranean.
They are caught easily by hand or by net.

The third remarkable event is
the appearance of *manna* (EXODUS 16:15).
(The word means "What is it?")
Could it be linked to sap
that oozes from certain desert shrubs
when insects puncture them?
Once exposed to the air,
it dries into a sweet, flaky food.

And so the question arises: How do we
explain these events? Were they

- *true miracles* worked by God,
- *ordinary events* that God used
  in an extraordinary way, or
- *literary symbols* expressing Israel's
  faith that God protected and guided them
  on their desert journey?

This much is certain. As the Israelites
meditated on their flight from Egypt
and their journey across the desert,
they realized they could not have made it
without God's special help.

How fully do I agree with this
statement of Alexander Yechaninov:
"Nothing in life is accidental.
He who believes in accidents
does not believe in God"?

Historians shake their heads:
"How did a band of ex-slaves,
with no organization and no education,
change the course of human history?"
For that is what the Israelites did.

The only explanation that makes sense
is the one they themselves gave.
At a mountain in the Sinai desert
they met God, who transformed them.

GOD   *I carried you*
           as an eagle carries
           her young on her wings,
           and brought you here to . . .
           be my chosen people, . . .
           and you will serve me
           as priests. . . .

NARRATOR   *On the morning*
           of the third day . . .
           a thick cloud appeared
           on the mountain, and . . .
           the people . . . trembled. . . .
           The LORD . . . called Moses to
           the top of the mountain.
                              EXODUS 19:4–6, 16, 20

Then God presents Moses
with these Ten Commandments:

[1.] Worship no god but me. . . .
[2.] Do not use my name for evil. . . .

[3.]   Keep [the Sabbath] holy. . . .
[4.]   Respect your [parents]. . . .
[5.]   Do not commit murder.
[6.]   Do not commit adultery.
[7.]   Do not steal.
[8.]   Do not accuse anyone falsely.
[9.]   Do not desire [another's wife]. . . .
[10.] Do not desire [another's property].
EXODUS 20:3, 7–8, 12–17

Moses wrote down
all the LORD's commands. . . .
The next morning, he built an altar. . . .
[After sacrificing cattle,
he read the commands to the people.
Then he poured blood on the altar and
on them, saying,] "This is the blood
that seals the covenant which
the LORD made with you." EXODUS 24:4, 8

And so at a mountain in the Sinai desert,
God transforms the Israelites dramatically,
giving them

- a new identity (Chosen People) and
- a new destiny (priestly people).

What are my thoughts
as I imagine myself to be an Israelite
participating in these historic events
at the foot of the mountain?

God's covenant with the people of Israel
followed a pattern
that was familiar to ancient peoples.
It paralleled the suzerainty treaties
of the time.

In these treaties,
a powerful king (suzerain) pledged
favors to a weaker king (vassal).
In turn the weaker king pledged
a total allegiance to the powerful king.

And so
God's covenant with the Israelites
transforms them, giving them

• a new identity (Chosen People) and
• a new destiny (priestly people).

Here's how Jewish writer Will Herberg
describes God's covenant with Israel in
Jewish Existence and Survival:

Israel is not a "natural" nation;
it is, indeed, not a nation at all
like the nations of the world.

It is a supernatural community,
called into being by God
to serve his eternal purposes in history.
It is a community
created by God's special act of covenant,

first with Abraham . . .
then . . . with Israel collectively. . . .

Apart from the covenant,
Israel is nothing
and Jewish existence a mere delusion.
The covenant is at the very heart
of Jewish self-understanding
of its own reality.

And so the Israelites encounter God
at a specific point in time and
at a specific place on the planet.
This gives Judaism its uniqueness.

Apart from Christianity and Islam,
both of which owe their origin,
in part, to Israel, no other religion
came about as Israel's did.
Other religions spring from nature;
Israel's springs from an encounter
with God in history.

On what occasion
and in what very real sense
did God choose me and give me
a new identity and a new destiny?
How might I explain to another person
the new identity and the new destiny
that was given to me by God?

God's covenant introduced the Israelites
to two revolutionary changes
in the way they lived. It gave them

• a new life style and
• a new worship style.

The new *life style*
based itself on the Ten Commandments.
The Israelites cherished them
as a sign of God's special love for them.
Their attitude toward the commandments
is summed up in this prayer to God:

*How I love your law! . . .
How sweet is the taste
of your instructions—
sweeter even than honey! . . .
Your word is a lamp to guide me and
a light for my path.* PSALM 119:97, 103, 105

Moses placed the Ten Commandments
(inscribed on two stone tablets)
in a Covenant Box, or container, called
the Ark of the Covenant (EXODUS 25:10–22).

The Ark was then placed behind
a sacred curtain in a specially designed
sacred Tent (EXODUS 25:8, 26:1–36).

The Book of Exodus describes
what happened when Moses did this.

Then the cloud covered the Tent
and the dazzling light
of the LORD's presence filled it. . . .

The Israelites moved their camp
to another place only when the cloud
lifted from the Tent. EXODUS 40:34–36
It was called the Tent
of the LORD's presence. EXODUS 33:7

This brings us to the new *worship style*
of the Israelites.

Its daily focus was the sacred Tent
(future Jerusalem Temple).

Its yearly focus was the Passover.
Marking the start
of the Jewish religious year,
the Passover celebration lasted a week
and followed God's instructions to Moses
the final night in Egypt (EXODUS 12).

Another feast that typified
the new worship style of the Israelites
was Yom Kippur, a time of repentance
and seeking God's forgiveness.

How close to Israel's love
for God's law is my own love for it?
How do I seek God's forgiveness?

Moses and the people stayed
at Mount Sinai for about a year.
Then they set out across the desert
for the land that God had promised them.
The desert into which they traveled
was made up of three regions:

- stretches of dry sand,
  where nothing grows;
- expanses of rock,
  with a few springs of water;
- semiarid land, with enough
  vegetation to feed sheep and goats.

Almost from the beginning
the problems began to develop
both from *within* and from *without*.

From *within*, the Israelites grew weary
and complained to Moses, saying, "Our
strength is gone. There is nothing at all
to eat—nothing but this manna" (NUMBERS 11:6).
Next, rebels began to challenge
the leadership of Moses (NUMBERS 16:3–14).

From *without*, foreign kings refused
to let the Israelites and their flocks
pass through their lands (NUMBERS 20:14–21).

But with God's help,
Moses managed to hold things together.
And, finally, after forty years of testing,

the Israelites emerged from the desert
and pitched camp on the plateau of Moab.
Stretching out below them, as far as
the eye could see, was the Promised Land.

About the size of Vermont and
about the latitude of Georgia,
the heart of the land
was a ten-mile-wide fertile valley.
Over the western ridge of the valley
was the Mediterranean Sea,
with its elegant white-sand beaches.

At the north end of the valley lay
the Sea of Galilee, a fisherman's paradise.
Sixty-five airline miles south
was the Dead Sea.
Linking these seas was the Jordan River.

To the desert-weary Israelites,
the Promised Land
was a breath-taking, spectacular sight.

How do I explain these words:
"The trouble with people today is that
they want to get to the Promised Land
without passing through the desert"?
What motivates me
to keep struggling through the desert?

Moses assembles the people
for an important series of instructions
in preparation for entering the land.

He explains how their desert sojourn was
a time of testing and teaching, saying:

"Remember
how the LORD your God led you . . .
through the desert these past forty years,
sending hardships
to test [and] . . . to teach you
that you must not depend on bread alone
to sustain you, but on everything
that the LORD says." DEUTERONOMY 8:2–3

Then Moses
recites the words of this song:

"Jacob's descendants he . . . found . . .
wandering through the desert. . . .
He protected them and cared for them. . . .
Like an eagle teaching its young to fly,
catching them safely
on its spreading wings, the LORD kept Israel
from falling." DEUTERONOMY 32:9–11

Like Moses' own time in the desert,
the Israelites' time in the desert
served as a schoolroom, teaching them
about their infidelity and weakness
and God's fidelity and power.

The Book of Deuteronomy ends
with the death of Moses.

The LORD buried him in a valley in Moab,
opposite the town of Bethpeor,
but to this day no one knows the exact
place of his burial. DEUTERONOMY 34:6

It is one of the ironies of history
that great leaders
who fight so valiantly for causes
often die without enjoying the results
of their struggles. Moses is an example.

The death of Moses concludes
the Jewish *Torah*, the name we give
to the first five books of the Bible:

- Genesis,
- Exodus,
- Leviticus,
- Numbers, and
- Deuteronomy.

These five books form the foundation
upon which the rest of the Bible is built.

What are my thoughts
as I imagine myself to be Moses,
realizing that my life is over?

God still calls people in modern times
"to go into the desert."
The call usually takes one of two forms:

- a permanent calling or
- a temporary "retreat."

First, consider the permanent calling.
Someone who felt it is Carlo Carretto.
Like Abraham of old,
Carlo felt called
to leave behind his former life
and to pursue a totally new one.
In *Letters from the Desert*, Carlo says:

God's call is mysterious;
it comes in the darkness of faith.
It is so fine, so subtle, that it is only
with the deepest silence within us
that we can hear it. . . .

When I was forty-four years old,
there occurred
the most serious call of my life:
the call to the contemplative life.
I experienced it deeply. . . .

"Leave everything
and come with me into the desert.
It is not
your acts and deeds that I want;
I want your prayer, your love."

Second, God's call "to go into the desert"
more often takes the form
of a "retreat" for a weekend or so.
The poet Carl Sandburg describes
such a retreat in these beautiful words:

[We] must get away now and then
to experience loneliness. Only those
who learn how to live with loneliness
can come to know themselves and life.
I go out there and walk
and look at the trees and sky.
I listen to the sounds of loneliness.
I sit on a rock or a stump
and say to myself,
"Who are you, Sandburg?
Where have you been,
and where are you going?"

And so the same God
who called Israel into the desert
still calls people into the desert.
That call takes either the form of

- a permanent calling or
- a temporary retreat.

Have I ever experienced a call
"to go into the desert"? What kind?
How is daily prayer a kind of temporary
"retreat" into the desert?

95

4 World of David

Timeline (key dates—B.C.E.)
c. 1250   Israelites (in Canaan)
c. 1240   Judges
c. 1020   Saul
c. 1000   David
c. 962   Solomon
c. 922   Division (Judah, Israel)

Bible (key books)

Joshua	1 Chronicles
Judges	2 Chronicles 1–9
Ruth	Psalms (early)
1–2 Samuel	Proverbs (early)
1 Kings 1–11	Song of Songs

MEDITERRANEAN
SEA

ASHER

NAPHTALI

• Dan

MANASSEH
(EAST)

• Hazor

SEA OF
GALILEE

Mount Carmel ▲

ZEBULUN

ISSACHAR

Megiddo •

Jordan River

Shechem •

MANASSEH
(WEST)

GAD

EPHRAIM

BENJAMIN

DAN

Jerusalem •

Bethlehem •

REUBEN

PHILISTINES

• Hebron

DEAD
SEA

JUDAH

Beersheba •

MOAB

SIMEON

When a chief is raised up,
he is told,
"Now you are poorer than any of us
because you have lost yourself,
you have become the nation's."
HAZEL DEAN-JOHN, Seneca clan mother

This happens to Joshua.
He is raised up to lead the Israelites.
Immediately he readies them to cross
the Jordan into the Promised Land.
The first to cross the river are priests,
carrying the Ark of the Covenant.

As soon as [they] stepped into the river,
the water stopped flowing. JOSHUA 3:15

This remarkable episode makes us ask,
Could an earthquake
have dammed the river temporarily?
The question is not out of line,
because the river lies on an earth fault.
An earthquake in 1927 killed hundreds.
And a landslide from that earthquake
blocked the Jordan River for a full day.

Whether or not this is the case when
the Israelites cross misses the point.
The point is clear. The episode affirms
that God is with the Israelites
as they cross the Jordan,
just as God was with their ancestors

as they crossed the Red (Reed) Sea.
In fact, the two crossings are related:

- Red Sea   marks Israel's exit
  from the land of slavery.
- Jordan River   marks Israel's entry
  into the land of freedom.

After Israel enters the land, Joshua
prepares to go into Jericho. He is told:

*"March around the city seven times
while the priests blow the trumpets.
Then they are to sound one long note.
As soon as you hear it,
all the people are to give a loud shout,
and the city walls will collapse."* JOSHUA 6:4–5

Joshua obeys and the walls collapse.
Again, is an earthquake involved?
Again, the question is not out of line.
Archaeologists have shown
that earlier in Jericho's history
an earthquake did destroy its walls.

After Jericho falls, Joshua attacks other
cities and eventually secures the land.

*What is Frederick Buechner's point
when he says, "Faith in God is less apt
to proceed from miracles
than miracles from faith in God"?*

[The Israelites] killed everyone
in the city [of Jericho],
men and women, young and old.
They also killed the cattle. JOSHUA 6:21

This kind of mass killing,
called "the ban," was not uncommon
among ancient peoples.
Although it shocks us, we need
only recall the Nazi holocaust of the Jews.
This modern atrocity does not justify
"the ban," but it does sober our outrage.

More to the point, "the ban" helps us
appreciate Israel's limited understanding
of God in the early stages of her history.
It is a highly primitive understanding
that will take centuries of clarification
under the prophets to mature.

For the present,
Israel thinks of God as a "national God."
As other nations have "protector gods,"
Israel has Yahweh.
And an enemy of Yahweh's people
is an enemy of Yahweh.

We also need to recall
that at this early time in her history,
Israel has no idea of an afterlife.
This will come later.

Until then, Israel assumes
that Yahweh executes judgment
upon the wicked in *this* life.
To chastise an enemy of Yahweh
is to act as an instrument of Yahweh.
It is a noble occupation.

And so the portrait of God
in the Book of Joshua must be interpreted
within the context of the times and
within the context of Israel's
primitive understanding of God:

- Yahweh orders wars.
- Yahweh takes Israel's side.
- Yahweh destroys Israel's enemies.

Only with the passage of time
will this portrait fill out in full color
and undergo dramatic refinement
by the prophets.

"God is inexpressible.
It is easier for us to say
what God is not than what God is. . . .
Nothing is comparable to God.
If you could conceive of God,
you would conceive
of something other than God." SAINT AUGUSTINE
How do I conceive of God
when I pray the Lord's Prayer?

Archaeologists have excavated
a number of the ancient city sites
mentioned in the Book of Joshua.
Their location is not too hard to spot.
They assume the appearance of a hill
standing on a plain.

Called a *tell*, the hill is the graveyard
of long-destroyed cities.
Wind, sand, vegetation, and the centuries
have buried them, giving them
their symmetrical appearance.

To understand how a tell develops,
we need to know that when fire or war
destroyed an ancient city,
the debris was not carted away.

People leveled the destroyed city
(often made of adobe huts)
and built on top of it.
The walls of the destroyed city
were simply built a little higher,
thus containing the tell as it grew.

Some tells contain a dozen layers,
meaning the debris of a dozen cities
is piled up there in pancake fashion.

For example, the University of Chicago
uncovered twenty layers in the
thirteen-acre tell at Megiddo (KINGS 9:15).

So many battles occurred at Megiddo
that the Book of Revelation makes it
the symbolic site of the end-time battle
between good and evil on earth.

The Book of Revelation calls the site
Armageddon (Har Megiddo),
meaning "Mount Megiddo" (REVELATION 16:16).

One of the first things archaeologists
look for in a tell is pottery.
Called the "alphabet of archaeology,"
pottery does not decay,
assumes many different shapes,
and contains a variety of designs.

The shapes and designs of pottery
are studied carefully by archaeologists.
Thus when pottery is found,
archaeologists are able to date it
with remarkable accuracy.
Its shape, style, and design
put it in a definite period of history.

*Nobel prize winner Albert Einstein said,
"Science without religion is lame;
religion without science is blind."
What was he probably referring to?
How might his statement also
apply to archaeology and the Bible?*

What happens when a leader dies
without a successor? This happens
to the Israelites when Joshua dies.
Without a leader, they flounder.
They drift away from the covenant
and even turn to false gods.

When this happens, God corrects them
by letting their enemies defeat them.
This brings the Israelites to their senses.
They repent and return to God.

We find this process repeating itself
over and over in the Book of Judges.
We might compare it to a play in four acts:
Israel sins, God corrects, Israel repents,
God forgives.

Here is an example to help illustrate
the fourfold process followed in Judges:

ACT 1   *The people of Israel sinned*
         against the LORD. . . .

ACT 2   *So the LORD let them*
         be conquered by Jabin,
         a Canaanite king [of Hazor].

ACT 3   *Then the people of Israel*
         cried out to the LORD. . . .

ACT 4   *Deborah . . . was serving*
         as a judge for the Israelites. . . .
         She sent for Barak. . . .

*Deborah said to Barak,
"Go! The L*ORD *. . .
has given you victory!"*
JUDGES 4:1–4, 6, 14

The name *Deborah* introduces us
to charismatic leaders called judges.
They are not black-robed figures
who sit in courtrooms and try cases.

Rather, they are gifted natural leaders
who surface from time to time
to defend Israel, uphold her honor, and
lead the people back to God.

Not all the judges are saintly people.
They are products of their time.
God uses them in spite of their sins.
Among the other judges are Gideon,
Jephthah, and Samson (JUDGES 6–8, 11, 13–16).

The role of judges, therefore,
is to provide some degree of leadership
from the death of Joshua
to the Era of the Kings.
The Era of the Judges extends roughly
from 1240 B.C.E. to 1040 B.C.E.

*As I look back over my life, to what extent
does it resemble the four-act pattern
of the Book of Judges?*

When the Era of the Judges ends,
Israel is without leadership.
The Bible says, "Everyone did
whatever they pleased" (JUDGES 21:25).
Into this leadership void stepped Samuel.
(Two books of the Bible bear his name.)
He anoints Saul, Israel's first king.

Saul starts brilliantly,
but success turns his head
and he drifts from God (1 SAMUEL 15:10–11).
Saul ends up as one of the tragic figures
of Old Testament history.

As the star of Saul falls in the sky,
the star of David rises (1 SAMUEL 16:1–13).
In time, he succeeds Saul as king.
Under David's dynamic leadership,
Israel begins its "years of lightning."

David makes Jerusalem his capital,
brings the Ark of the Covenant there,
and lays plans to build
a beautiful temple for the Ark.
But one night the LORD reveals to David
that the honor of building the temple
will fall to his son, adding:

You will always have descendants, and
I will make your kingdom last forever.
Your dynasty will never end. 2 SAMUEL 7:16

This covenant promise to David
is one of the milestones in the Bible.
It begins a series of promises
known as the "messianic prophecies."
They point to a messiah ("anointed one")
from David's line,
whose Kingdom (God's) will never end.

And so just as God's covenant changed
Abraham and Israel, it now changes David.
The changes follow this pattern:

Abraham is given
- a new identity: *chosen person*, and
- a new destiny: *father of many.*

Israel is given
- a new identity: *chosen people,* and
- a new destiny: *priestly people.*

David is given
- a new identity: *chosen king,* and
- a new destiny: *Messiah's ancestor.*

*"In the Old Testament,
the New Testament lies concealed;
in the New Testament,
the Old Testament lies revealed."* SAINT AUGUSTINE
What is Augustine's point?
Can I think of an example to illustrate it?

David is credited
with authoring the Book of Psalms.
Actually, he probably wrote
only a few of its 150 entries.
Ancients commonly credited authorship
to a person who began or promoted
a literary undertaking.

The Book of Psalms plays a twofold role
in Israel's worship life.
It is its prayer book and its hymnbook.

As Israel's *prayer book,*
it gives us a glimpse into Israel's soul.
We see how the people pray to God
in times of doubt, sorrow, and joy.

As Israel's *hymnbook,*
it gives us a glimpse into Israel's heart.
We see how the people celebrate,
especially in two settings.

The *first setting* is around a campfire.
A musician begins by strumming
a musical instrument; and the people—
especially the children—
join in, clapping, dancing, and singing.

Listen [to the marvelous things] . . .
our ancestors told us.
We will not keep them from

our children; we will tell [them] . . .
about the LORD's power and
his great deeds. PSALM 78:1, 3–4

The *second setting* is the Temple,
especially on Jewish holy days.
Temple worship included
instrumental music, song, and dance.
It involved a chorus, dancers, musicians,
and the whole congregation.

Psalm 150 gives us an insight into it.
The psalm takes only seconds to read
but took, perhaps, an hour to perform.

To catch its spirit, imagine a director
inviting each music group
to praise the LORD in its unique way:

Praise [the LORD] with trumpets.
Praise [the LORD] with harps and lyres.
Praise [the LORD] with drums and dancing.
Praise [the LORD] with harps and flutes.
Praise [the LORD] with cymbals. . . .
Praise [the LORD], all living creatures!
                                        PSALM 150:3–6

What are my thoughts
as I imagine myself to be an Israelite
in the Temple on a major feast day,
participating in the celebration?

Solomon became king upon David's death.
Shrewd in politics and finance,
Solomon made Israel strong and wealthy.
But power and prosperity took their toll.
Solomon's early idealism (1 KINGS 8)
turned to decadence (1 KINGS 11).

Because Solomon is known, especially,
for his wisdom, he is credited
with authoring three wisdom books:

- Proverbs,
- Song of Songs,
- Ecclesiastes.

First, consider the Book of Proverbs.
Every nation has its proverbs.
Cervantes describes a proverb as a
"short sentence based on long experience."
Lord Russell describes it as
"the wisdom of many and the wit of one."

The purpose of Israel's Book of Proverbs
is to teach the young, especially,
"how to live intelligently and how to be
honest, just, and fair" (PROVERBS 1:3).
For example, one proverb reads:

*If you refuse to listen to the cry
of the poor, your own cry for help
will not be heard.* PROVERBS 21:13

Second, consider the Song of Songs.
It takes the form of a love poem.
An excerpt reads:

Come then, my love;
my darling, come with me.
The winter is over; . . .
the flowers are in bloom.
This is the time for singing;
the song of the doves is heard. . . .
Come then, my love;
my darling, come with me.
SONG OF SONGS 2:10–13

Some scholars speculate that the poem
was used as part of a marriage rite.
The groom's love for his bride
symbolizes God's love for Israel.

Thus the poem has two levels of meaning.
On the surface,
it describes the love of two people.
At a deeper level,
it describes God's love for Israel.

We will consider Ecclesiastes later.

What are my thoughts as I reflect on
the above excerpt from the Song of Songs
and imagine God speaking it to me?

5 World of Prophets

Weeks

8	Division
9	Rebirth

Timeline (key dates—B.C.E)

922	Jeroboam
922	Rehoboam
976–850	Omri and Ahab
722	North falls
715–687	Hezekiah
640–609	Josiah
587–539	Exile
168–142	Maccabees
63–37	Romans
37–4	Herod

Bible (key books)

1–2 Kings	Jeremiah
2 Chronicles 10–31	Ezekiel
Amos	Jonah
Hosea	Job
Isaiah	Ecclesiastes
Micah	Daniel

Native Americans in South Dakota
were once forced to live in dire poverty.
The reservation had no employment,
and the nearest public transportation
was thirty miles away.
People wanted to work but couldn't.

Tragic situations like this explain
why people sometimes turn to violence
to try to right the wrongs of injustice.
This happens in Israel after Solomon dies
and his son, Rehoboam, takes the throne.

Solomon has taxed the people heavily
to support his building projects.
Thus, when Rehoboam becomes king,
the ten northern tribes, led by Jeroboam,
band together to change this (1 KINGS 12:1–24).
But their pleas fall on deaf ears;
and so, in 922 B.C.E., the twelve tribes
split into two rival nations:

- Israel in the north and
- Judah in the south.

To keep people in the north from going
south to worship at the Temple
in Jerusalem, the south sets up
religious centers at Bethel and Dan.
This plants the seeds
of religious disunity and idolatry.

The seeds germinate and sprout when,
years later, Ahab becomes Israel's king.
He marries a pagan princess, Jezebel,
who openly promotes the cult
of the pagan storm god, Baal.

Because Baal is supposed to be in charge
of the fertility of flocks and fields,
he appeals to Israelite farmers—
especially when Yahweh seems to ignore
their prayers in times of drought.

Baal ministers exploit the situation,
telling Israelite shepherds and farmers,
"Yahweh is a desert god, not a farm god."
The result is tragic, fueling the flames of

- religious disunity and
- religious idolatry.

Into this critical situation steps a group
of spiritual giants called *prophets*.
With their appearance a new era dawns
in the history of God's people.

*"Fight all error, but do it with good humor,
patience, kindness, and love.
Harshness will damage your own soul
and spoil the best cause."* SAINT JOHN OF KANTY
How do I fight error?

Tourists entering Palestine
by the seaport of northern Haifa
can see Mount Carmel from the ship.
At Mount Carmel, the prophet Elijah and
450 prophets of Baal held a contest
to determine the "true God."

The Baal prophets began the contest
by placing a young bull on an altar.
Then they prayed to Baal, their "storm god,"
to strike the bull with lightning
and set it ablaze.
When nothing happened,
Elijah taunted them.

ELIJAH   *Pray louder! . . .*
                Maybe Baal's sleeping. . . .

NARRATOR   *The prophets prayed louder*
                and cut themselves
                with knives . . .
                but no answer came. . . .
                [Then, Elijah took over.]

ELIJAH   *O LORD, the God of Abraham,*
                Isaac, and Jacob, [answer] . . .
                so that this people will know
                that you, the LORD, are God. . . .

NARRATOR   *The LORD sent fire and*
                it burned up the sacrifice. . . .
                When the people saw this,
                they . . . exclaimed, "The LORD
                is God." 1 KINGS 18:27–29, 36–39

This story of Elijah
and other stories like it (1 KINGS 17, 19)
serve an important twofold purpose.
They teach the people that they should
worship Yahweh alone and
have faith in Yahweh, as Elijah did.

Elijah's colorful ministry ends abruptly
when he is taken to heaven
in a "chariot of fire" (2 KINGS 2:11).
Symbolic or not, this striking story
of Elijah's exit from earth gives rise
to the belief that he will return
(MALACHI 4:5, MATTHEW 17:12).

Elisha continues Elijah's ministry.
Like his teacher Elijah,
he is credited with great wonders,
even raising the dead (2 KINGS 4:32–37).
And, like Elijah,
Elisha is remembered and eulogized
by none other than Jesus (LUKE 4:25–27).

Without the prophets,
there would be no apostles or martyrs.
For it was the prophets
who kept the "flame of faith" burning
when it flickered and almost went out.
What am I doing to keep faith alive
in my own era of human history,
in my own sphere of influence?

Decades ago an eastern city lady
asked a remote western motel clerk
about the weather for the next day.
The clerk had no information.
A Native American guide,
sitting nearby,
heard her and said, "Rain! Much rain!"

The next day, the rain poured down.
Awed by the guide's accuracy,
the lady inquired again the next day.
"Blue sky! Cold air!" he replied.
Again, the prediction was correct.
The next night,
the lady consulted him again.
"Dunno!" he replied. "Radio broke!"

The prophets were much like that guide.
Their message wasn't their own either.
It came from a higher source: God.
The prophets fall into two main groups:

- nonwriting, like Elijah, and
- writing, so called because
  their writings appear in books
  that bear their name.

The *writing* prophets divide
into two main groups:

- major ones (long writings) and
- minor ones (short writings).

The four major prophets are:

Isaiah   Ezekiel
Jeremiah   Daniel

The twelve minor prophets are:

Hosea   Jonah   Zephaniah
Joel   Micah   Haggai
Amos   Nahum   Zechariah
Obadiah   Habbakuk Malachi

Included among the *prophetic* writings
are two other books (linked to Jeremiah):
Baruch and Lamentations.

Prophets and kings often traveled in tandem,
because one of the prophet's jobs was
to counsel and to confront the king.
Thus they had a twofold role. They were:

- *foretellers:*   they counseled, and
- *forthtellers:* they confronted.

Nathan is an example. He counseled David
about God's promise (2 SAMUEL 7:1–17)
and confronted him about sin (2 SAMUEL 12:1–12).

*"The prophet is appointed to oppose
the king, and even more: history."* MARTIN BUBER
*In what sense is a follower of Jesus
appointed to be a prophet in our world?*

119

A cartoon shows a bearded old man
holding a sign that reads:
"Repent! The end is near!"
Behind him, rockets crisscross the sky.
The caption reads: "Have you noticed?
No one's laughing at him anymore!"

Biblical prophets were often treated that
way—rejected or ridiculed. Take Amos.

God called him from his farm in Judah
to be the first writing prophet to Israel.
He was sent to the temple of Bethel
to confront the northern kingdom
about social injustices toward the poor.

Pointing a bony finger
at the rich and the powerful, Amos says,
"[God says,] 'They trample down the weak . . .
and push the poor out of the way'" (AMOS 2:7).

And to those who sing loud songs to God
on the Sabbath but oppress God's poor
the rest of the week, Amos shouts,
"[God says,] 'Stop your noisy songs. . . .
Instead, let justice flow like a stream,
and righteousness like a river'" (AMOS 5:23–24).

The reaction to Amos is predictable.
He is driven out of town (AMOS 7:12).
Amos returns to Judah, but not before
making the same point that

the New Testament writer John makes
years later: "If we say we love God,
but hate others, we are liars" (1 JOHN 4:20).

Amos is followed by the prophet Hosea.
Little is known of him except that he marries
an unfaithful wife but remains
faithful to her—as God stays faithful
to unfaithful Israel (HOSEA 3:1–5).

Hosea takes a more tender approach.
He reminds the Israelites
of God's love for them.
Speaking in God's name, he says:

"When Israel was a child, I . . .
called him out of Egypt as my son.
But the more I called to him,
the more he turned from me." HOSEA 11:1–2

But neither Amos's bluntness
nor Hosea's tenderness moved Israel.

"The food you have stored away
belongs to the hungry;
the unworn garment in your closet
belongs to the naked;
the gold you have hidden away
belongs to the poor." SAINT BASIL (fourth century)
What might be the reaction of a
congregation to Amos or Basil?

In his novel *The Power and the Glory*,
Graham Greene describes a priest
who lives in Mexico
during a time of religious persecution.
Fear of being caught takes its toll;
and the priest becomes an alcoholic,
is caught, and sentenced to death.

On the morning of his execution he wakes
with an empty brandy flask in his hand.
He tries to pray but is too confused.

Then he notices his shadow on the wall.
He stares at it for a minute.
Tears roll down his cheeks.
He is crying not because he is afraid
but because he has to go to God
so empty-handed.
At that moment he'd have given anything
to be able to relive his life.

Such a moment comes for Israel.
In spite of Elijah and Elisha,
in spite of Amos and Hosea,
the North does not change its ways.

And so the Day of the Lord dawns,
a day without brightness (AMOS 5:20).
In 722 B.C.E. the Assyrians conquer Israel.
What the prophets tried to avoid
now comes to pass.

Most of the people are led away
and never heard from again. Historians
call them the "lost tribes" of Israel.

A few inhabitants, however,
are permitted to remain behind.
But their fate falls under a shadow.
They intermarry with the Assyrians.
This draws down upon them
the contempt of other Jews.
The Samaritans, as they were called,
are never again respected by most Jews.

Shock waves rumble through Judah
when they hear of Israel's fate.
But they do not panic, smugly thinking
that no such tragedy can befall them.
Aren't they ruled by David's line?
Aren't they heirs to God's promise
of an unending kingdom?

Ironically, Judah soon drifts
into the same evils that befell Israel:

- idolatry,
- religious formalism (going through
  the motions of worship), and
- exploitation of the poor.

How complacent am I about my faith?

No prophet is more admired by Jews and Christians than Isaiah. Called "the prophet of God's holiness," his forty-year-long ministry begins with a vision. He writes:

ISAIAH   *I saw the LORD.*
         He was sitting on his throne,
         high and exalted. . . .
         Flaming creatures [called] . . .
         "Holy, holy, holy!
         The LORD Almighty is holy! . . ."
LORD   *Whom shall I send? . . .*
ISAIAH   *I will go! Send me!*
         So he told me to go.   ISAIAH 6:1–3, 8–9

Isaiah confronts Judah, saying:

"You are stained red with sin,
but I will wash you as clean as snow. . . .
But if you defy me, you are doomed to die.
I, the LORD, have spoken."   ISAIAH 1:18, 20

One of Isaiah's warnings takes the form of a parable expressed in song:

I sing . . . of my friend and his vineyard. . . .
He waited for the grapes to ripen,
but every grape was sour.
So now my friend says, . . .
"I will let briers and thorns cover it. . . ."
Israel is the vineyard . . . ;
the people of Judah are the vines.   ISAIAH 5:1–3, 6–7

Isaiah's warnings go unheeded.
It is clear that only a shock will get
Judah to reform. It comes in 701 B.C.E.

Assyrian armies under Sennecherib
march in battle array toward Jerusalem.
When they reach the city walls,
they pitch camp
and prepare for battle in the morning.

As night falls,
King Hezekiah and all of Jerusalem
crouch terrified inside the city walls.
The next morning, when the sun rises,
they can hardly believe what they see.
The Assyrians are pulling out.

After the Assyrians depart,
patrols go out and find the site littered
with bodies: a plague had struck the
Assyrian camp (2 KINGS 19:35, SIRACH 48:21).

You would think this narrow escape
would have shocked Judah into reform.
But it didn't.

*What are my thoughts as I imagine
myself to be part of the patrol and find
the Assyrian camp littered with bodies?*

Tragedy hits Judah after Hezekiah dies
and his son Manesseh takes the throne.
Ruling for over thirty years, he proves
to be one of Judah's worst kings.
The Second Book of Kings says of him,
"He practiced . . . magic and consulted
fortunetellers" (2 KINGS 21:6).

No tears are shed when he finally dies
and the throne passes
to Josiah, an eight-year-old boy.
Josiah grows up to be remarkable.

In his twenties, he remodels the Temple.
During the work,
an old book of the law is found.
When it is read to Josiah, he tears
his clothes "in dismay" (2 KINGS 22:11).
Josiah orders an immediate reform.
An array of prophets back him:
Nahum, Zephaniah, Habakkuk, Jeremiah.

Of these, Jeremiah is the giant.
Like Josiah, he is called at a young age.
At first he protests that he is too young.
But God has other plans. Jeremiah says:

The LORD reached out, touched my lips,
and said to me, . . . "I give you authority
over nations." JEREMIAH 1:9–10

Reform begins and proceeds.

Then Josiah is killed,
leaving Jeremiah to pursue reform alone.
He stations himself outside the Temple
and warns the people:

"Change the way you are living. . . .
Be fair in your treatment
of one another. . . .
Stop worshiping other gods." JEREMIAH 7:5–6

Pointing his finger
in the direction of Babylon, he warns,
"Your enemies are coming" (JEREMIAH 13:20).
But the people ignore his words.
Finally the time comes when Jeremiah
must pass sentence on those he loves.

Enraged, the people throw him into a pit.
Brutal treatment like this
wounds Jeremiah's sensitive
nature.
Once again, he protests to God:

I am ridiculed and scorned . . .
because I proclaim your message. . . .
Curse the day I was born! JEREMIAH 20:8, 14

What are my thoughts
as I imagine myself to be Jeremiah,
imprisoned in a pit,
rejected by my own people,
and abandoned by God?

Jeremiah's warnings become bitter reality.
In 597 B.C.E. Babylonian armies attack
and conquer Judah, carrying off in tribute
skilled artisans and precious treasures.

But the city and the Temple survive.
The king and the people
regard their survival as a sign
of God's special protection.
But Jeremiah sees it differently—
as a warning from God.
If Judah ignores the warning,
terrible things will happen (JEREMIAH 22:5).

Tragically, Judah ignores the warning
and terrible things happen.
In 587 B.C.E. Babylonian armies return,
destroy Jerusalem and the Temple, and
take the people prisoner (JEREMIAH 39:1-10).

The people are divided into three groups.
First, there are the very poor,
left behind to grub for themselves.
Second, there are the refugees,
who flee to Egypt, Jeremiah among them.
Third, there are the talented citizens:
those skilled in arts and crafts.
They are exiled as prisoners to Babylon.

With their exile, the focus of the history
of God's Chosen People shifts from
Jerusalem to Babylon.

Some of the exiles drift from their faith
and fall into Babylonian ways.
But others remain faithful to God or,
in other cases, undergo a conversion
as a result of what has happened.

Faithful and converted Jews meet
each Sabbath to ponder God's word.
Out of these Sabbath meetings emerge
two unexpected blessings.

First, a new worship place emerges.
Called the synagogue,
it is primarily a *place of instruction*.
It differs from the Temple,
which is primarily a *place of sacrifice*.

Second, the written word of God emerges.
Scribes begin to record God's word,
most of which had been passed on orally.

As these faithful Jews reach up to God,
God reaches down to them,
sending prophets like Ezekiel and
Second Isaiah—as we will soon see.

*"The more we depend on God,
the more dependable we find God is."*
CLIFF RICHARDS
How dependable do I find God?

Today, the ancient city of Babylon
has been excavated from a sandy grave.
For the first time in centuries,
the sun shines on its ancient ruins.
Through the city's famous Isthar Gate,
proud Babylonian armies
used to parade their trophies of war.

Through this same gate walked Ezekiel,
the first of two great prophets.
Reared in Jerusalem,
it is there that he receives God's call.
His ministry divides into two periods:
before the fall of Jerusalem and
after the fall.

Before the fall, Ezekiel is a *disturber,*
warning the people about
their complacency over their situation.
After the fall, he is the *comforter,*
prophesying the eventual restoration
of the king (EZEKIEL 34:23), the people
(EZEKIEL 37:14), and the Temple (EZEKIEL 43:5-7).

New Testament writers see Jesus
fulfilling these three prophecies:

- king   Jesus is the Good Shepherd,
            the *eternal king* (JOHN 10:11);
- nation   Jesus sends the Holy Spirit,
            who forms his followers
            into a *holy people* (ACTS 2);

- temple   Jesus' followers become
God's new *living temple*
(1 CORINTHIANS 3:16–17).

But the New Testament and Jesus
are far beyond the horizon in the future.
All that faithful Jews can do now
is wait in darkness with a candle of hope.

The second prophet of the Babylonian exile
is "Second Isaiah,"
so called by many because he prophesies
in the spirit of "great" Isaiah.

Eventually his writings are appended
to those of "great" Isaiah
and called the Book of Consolation (40–55).
The following passage echoes its spirit:

Those who trust in the LORD for help
will find their strength renewed.
They will rise on wings like eagles;
they will run and not get weary;
they will walk and not grow weak.

ISAIAH 40:31

"Never fear shadows.
They simply mean there's light
shining somewhere nearby."

RUTH RENKLE

What are some shadows that I see right now?

131

*When can I go
and worship in your presence?* PSALM 42:2

For five decades Jews sit in darkness,
hoping and praying.
Then one day, rumors begin to circulate.
The armies of King Cyrus of Persia
are marching across the land,
piling up victory after victory.

"Is it possible?" Jews wonder.
Will the armies of Cyrus invade Babylon?
Will Cyrus be the instrument
by which Yahweh will reassert
a saving presence in Israel's history?
As the rumors mount,
so do the hopes of the excited Jews.

Finally, Second Isaiah sings out:

*"Comfort my people," says our God. . . .
"They have suffered long enough. . . ."
To Cyrus the LORD says, . . .
"I appoint you to help my servant Israel,
the people that I have chosen. . . .
I will send victory . . . like rain;
the earth . . . will blossom with freedom
and justice."* ISAIAH 40:1–2; 45:1, 4, 8

And so after long years of waiting,
Yahweh is about to act decisively,

just as Yahweh did for their ancestors
long ago in Egypt.

The exiled Jews
will cross the desert in a "new exodus."
Second Isaiah sings joyfully:

"Prepare . . . a road for the LORD!
Clear the way in the desert for our God!"
ISAIAH 40:3

Finally, the great day dawns.
Cyrus invades Babylon, and the city falls.
An ancient record, the "Cyrus Cylinder,"
says he entered the city "as a friend."

Immediately Cyrus issues a proclamation
giving Jews permission to go home
to rebuild their city and Temple (EZRA 1:3).

It is too fantastic to be true.
The joy of the Jews reaches fever pitch.
The psalmist recalls the great moment:

It was like a dream! How we laughed,
how we sang for joy! PSALM 126:1–2

What are some of my thoughts
as I imagine myself
to be an elderly Jew preparing to leave
for the trip back to Jerusalem?

A white and gray Starlifter, filled with
American POWs returning from Vietnam,
touched down on a runway in 1973.
A huge crowd surged forward, chanting,
"Welcome home, welcome home!"

No such welcome greeted the
Jewish POWs returning from Babylon—
only the empty echo of the deserted city.
Years of rebuilding—under leaders
like Ezra and Nehemiah and prophets
like Haggai and Zechariah—lay ahead.

Top priority is given to the Temple.
Samaritans offer to help the returnees,
but are told to leave (NEHEMIAH 4:1–9).
Angered, the Samaritans turn hostile
and hinder rather than help (NEHEMIAH 4:16–18).

Further problems develop when
farm crops fail during the first season.
Enthusiasm turns sour,
and the returnees turn inward, shrinking
their vision and isolating themselves.
They forget they are God's instruments,
chosen for the re-creation of the world.
Into this critical situation
step two prophets: Malachi and Jonah.

Jonah's message, especially, stands out.
Literalists interpret the Book of Jonah

factually; contextualists, *symbolically,*
as a kind of book-length parable.

God orders Jonah to go to Nineveh
and preach repentance to the people.
Jonah can't believe his ears.
The Ninevites are enemies and sinners.
They should be smashed, not saved.
So he flees from God on a ship to Spain.

A storm at sea washes Jonah overboard.
He is swallowed by a great fish
and spit up on a deserted beach.
God appears again and repeats the order:
"Preach to the Ninevites!"
Jonah obeys and the Ninevites repent.

The point of the Jonah story is clear.
It confronts the people of Judah
and reminds them that God is concerned
about all people, not just Jews.

The Book of Jonah
reveals a new universalism concerning
God's saving activity in human history.
God is not a "tribal" God for Judah alone,
but the "universal" God of all peoples.

*Do I tend to look upon certain people
as Jonah did——as enemies I want to smash,
not as people God wants to save?*

135

*I have seen everything . . . ,
and I tell you, it is all useless.
It is like chasing the wind.* ECCLESIASTES 1:14

Jews feel the same way
in the years following their rebuilding
of Jerusalem and the Temple.

They are occupied and controlled
by one powerful nation after another.
This pawnlike existence jolts their pride
and shatters their dreams of someday
being a glorious nation with a great king.

Their discouragement and confusion
are reflected in the Book of Ecclesiastes.
It contains none of the sure-footed
wisdom of the Book of Proverbs.
And this is where its value lies.
It mirrors the heart of a Jew
waiting for further revelation from God.

For example, Jews had little or no idea
of reward or punishment in an afterlife.
They assumed
God rewards and punishes in *this* life.
But this doesn't always happen. Why?

This is the question
raised in the Book of Job.
Job spends his whole life doing good.
He is a saint if there ever was one.

Then tragedy after tragedy befall him.
Job cannot understand! Why?

When Job has probed all possibilities
without an answer, a storm blows up.
Out of the storm, God's voice comes,
asking Job a series of questions:

"Was it you, Job,
who made horses so strong? . . .
Does a hawk learn from you how to fly? . . .
Does an eagle wait for your command
to build its nest?" JOB 39:19, 26–27

Gradually the point dawns on Job—
the same point Isaiah made years ago.
To doubt God's fairness or wisdom
is to be a fool, not a person of faith.

"As high as the heavens are
above the earth, so high are my ways
and thoughts above yours." ISAIAH 55:9

"Reason can lead us
to the base of the mountain,
but only faith can lift us to the top."
ANONYMOUS

Do I ever question God's fairness
and wisdom? How do I strive to keep
my balance between faith and reason?

Week 9: **Rebirth**

Day 6: **Call to Trust**

People who play God are dangerous.
Syrian King Antiochus IV was one of them.
Believing he was an incarnation
of the Greek god Zeus,
he called himself *Epiphanes* ("god-seen").
Jews called him *Epimanes* ("madman").

Antiochus conquered Judah
around 200 B.C.E.
and tried to turn Jews into Greeks.
Result? A religious persecution
broke out that shook Judah to its roots.
The Book of Daniel
addresses this horrendous situation.
It divides into two major sections:

- stories about a young Jew, Daniel,
  who remains faithful to God
  during the Babylonian exile, and
- visions that God gives to Daniel.

Typical of the *stories* is one about
Daniel's appointment to serve
in the palace of the Babylonian king.
Babylonian court officials envy Daniel
because he is highly respected by the king.

Aware that Daniel prays to God daily,
the officials connive to have the king
pass a law forbidding prayer of this kind.
Of course, Daniel ignores the law.

Result? He is thrown to the lions,
which refuse to touch him.
The point of the story is to assure
persecuted Jews that God will save them,
as God saved Daniel in the lions' den.

Typical of Daniel's *visions*
is one in which he sees

One like a son of man coming,
on the clouds of heaven;
When he reached the Ancient One
and was presented before him,
He received dominion, glory, and kingship. . . .
His dominion is . . . everlasting . . . ,
his kingship shall not be destroyed.

DANIEL 7:13–14 (NAB)

Jesus cited this vision of Daniel
and applied it to himself, saying:

"You will all see the Son of Man
seated at the right side of the Almighty
and coming with the clouds of heaven!"

MARK 14:62

The title "Son of Man" (used of Jesus
seventy times in the New Testament)
alludes to Jesus' unique identity
as both "Son of God" and "Son of Man."

What might I say to Jesus about his identity?

139

Persecution of the Jews reaches
a turning point around 175 B.C.E.
Three Maccabee brothers
(Judas, Simon, and Jonathan)
organize a revolt against the Syrians.

Operating out of hills and ravines,
the revolutionaries fight for freedom.
Eventually Judas and Jonathan
are killed, but Simon brings the revolt
to a successful conclusion.

When Simon dies around 135 B.C.E.,
leadership passes to his son John.
This begins the Hasmonean Era.
(Hasmonean is the name given
to the descendants of the Maccabees.)
Sadly, politics enters religion in this era:
The office of high priest is used
to gain political goals.

The clock finally strikes midnight
for the Hasmoneans.
The Romans occupy Jerusalem in 63 B.C.E.
Hasmonean rule ends in 37 B.C.E.,
when the Romans crown
"Herod the Great" king of Judah.
It is this man, with so many talents
and so many weaknesses,
who serves as the bridge between
the Old Testament and the New Testament.

And so by their own admission,
the Hebrew Scriptures end "unfinished."
They end with faithful Jews,
especially "the poor,"
waiting and praying for the Messiah.

A fitting image of Jewish society
at this point in history is this one
from *The Source* by James Michener.
Rabbi Asher is strolling in an orchard.
Suddenly he spots an old olive tree.

Its interior was rotted away,
leaving an empty shell . . .
but somehow the remaining fragments
held contact with the roots,
and the old tree was still vital. . . .

Asher thought that it well summarized
the state of the Jewish people . . .
whose interior had rotted away,
but whose fragments
still held their vital connection
with the roots of God. . . .

[Through these roots]
Jews could ascertain the will of God
and produce good fruit.

How are a lot of people today
like Rabbi Asher's olive tree?

141

6 World of Jesus

Weeks

Timeline (key dates, traditional—C.E.)

1	Jesus' birth
30	Jesus' preaching
33	Jesus' resurrection

Bible (key books)

Matthew
Mark
Luke
John

MEDITERRANEAN
SEA

• Sidon

• Tyre

• Caesarea Philippi

Capernaum •

Cana • Tiberias • SEA OF
  • Nazareth   GALILEE
       ▲
     Mount Tabor

• Caesarea

SAMARIA

• Gerasa

Jordan River

• Joppa

Emmaus •
Jerusalem • Qumram
   • Bethlehem

JUDEA

DEAD
SEA

NABATEA

Nathaniel Hawthorne was dead.
On his desk lay the outline of a story
he never got a chance to write.
It concerns an important person
who is coming to a certain place.
People plan for his coming.
They wait for him, but he never comes.

The Old Testament is like
this story outlined by Hawthorne.
It centers around the promised Messiah.

The LORD says, "The time is coming
when I will choose as king
a . . . descendant of David . . . called
'The LORD Our Salvation.' " JEREMIAH 23:5–6

People plan for the Messiah.
They wait for him, but he never comes.

It is against this background
that we put down the Old Testament
and pick up the New Testament.

The Old Testament concerns
God's covenant with the *Jewish people,*
mediated through *Moses.*
The New Testament
concerns God's covenant with *all people,*
mediated through *Jesus.*
The New Testament
does not replace the Old Testament.

On the contrary, it fulfills it—
much as adulthood fulfills childhood.

And just as the Old Testament
is divided into four groups of books,
so the New Testament
is divided into four groups of books:

- Gospels   4 books
- Acts of the Apostles   1 book
- Letters   21 books
- Revelation   1 book

The gospels form the key group.
It announces the Good News
of the coming of the promised Messiah,
Jesus Christ, the Son of God.
The other three groups build on it.

- Acts tells how Jesus' followers
  preach the Good News to the world.
- Letters tells how they apply
  the Good News to their daily lives.
- Revelation tells how they suffer
  persecution for their faith in Jesus.

I imagine I am an elderly Jew,
living before Jesus' birth.
All my life I've waited for the Messiah.
What are my thoughts as I prepare
to die without any sign of his coming?

145

A science-fiction story
concerns a team of scientists
who develop an energy screen
that lets people
travel backward in time.

Imagine such an energy screen exists.
Imagine a TV crew
traveling backward to gospel times,
videotaping and computerizing
the entire life of Jesus.
By typing on a keyboard the name
of any event from the life of Jesus,
you can call it up on a TV screen.

Now, suppose you could trade
the *gospel version* of Jesus' life
for this spectacular *video version*.
But there's a catch!

If you make the trade,
the world will lose the *gospel version*.
In other words, future generations
will no longer have the four gospels.

Before reading further, ask yourself,
Would I make the trade?
Why? Why not?

The *video version* would be fantastic.
But it would leave us
with the same problem the disciples had.

Many of them saw and heard what Jesus said
and did, but they missed the point.

Thus if we had only a video of Jesus' life,
we might miss the point too.
For example, the disciples did not
understand Jesus' passion prophecy
(MARK 9:31-32). Nor did they understand
the Palm Sunday episode (JOHN 12:12-16).

What eventually happened to help
the disciples understand these things?
Exactly what Jesus had foretold:

"The Helper, the Holy Spirit,
whom the Father will send in my name,
will teach you everything
and make you remember
all that I have told you." JOHN 14:26

The Gospel is special because
it is written in the light
of the Spirit's coming on Pentecost.
It is this event that gives clarity
to the words and works of Jesus.
The Gospel according to John, especially,
reflects this fact (JOHN 2:22).

Can I recall an event in my life
that I didn't understand or appreciate
until much later?

147

A TV commercial for a camera
shows two young ladies talking together.
Suddenly someone snaps their picture.
Instantly a paper rolls from the camera.
But it's blank; nothing is on it.
Then the *light of the sun* hits it,
and it turns into a beautiful picture.

Some events in Jesus' life are like that.
At first they seem blank, meaningless,
but then the Holy Spirit comes.
When the *light of the Spirit* hits them,
they turn into beautiful pictures.
Describing the Spirit's coming, Luke writes:

When the day of Pentecost came,
all the believers were gathered together
in one place.
Suddenly . . . they saw
what looked like tongues of fire which
spread out and touched every person there.
They were all filled with the Holy Spirit.
ACTS 2:1–4

Jesus had foretold this event, saying:

"I have much more to tell you, but now
it would be too much for you to bear.
When, however, the Spirit comes,
who reveals the truth about God,
he will lead you into all truth." JOHN 16:12–13

And so the Spirit's coming sheds light
on the events of Jesus' life.
Thus, in a real sense,
the Gospel is born on Pentecost.

The disciples' first reaction is not
to sit down and *record* the "Good News."
It is to go out and *preach* it (ACTS 2:5ff).
With a burning urgency,
they carry it as far as Rome itself.

The reason for their urgency is that
they believe Jesus will return (ACTS 1:11)
after they have preached the Gospel
to all nations (MATTHEW 24:14).

In their excitement, they think
they can do this within their lifetime.
When they see this is impossible,
they arrange to have the Gospel recorded.
Peter writes:

I shall soon put off this mortal body. . . .
I will do my best, then,
to provide a way for you
to remember these matters
at all times after my death.   2 PETER 1:14–15

For what other reasons
did the disciples decide to record
the Gospel?   (GALATIANS 1:7, 2 PETER 3:16)

149

A famous painting shows an angel
bending over Matthew, guiding his hand.

The angel symbolizes the divine guidance
or "inspiration" that certifies
that the gospel Matthew is writing
is not an ordinary book. . . .
The problem with the painting's image
is not the value it seeks to communicate
but the process of composing the gospel
that it implies. DONALD SENIOR, *Jesus*

The evangelists
were more than robots or secretaries.
The process of recording the Gospel
is far more complex than that.
For example, divine guidance began
long before the biblical writer
picked up his pen to begin writing.

Many parables and stories in the Gospel
already had the form they now have
as a result of being preached
for so long a time by the disciples.

The four gospels, as we have them today,
passed through three stages
before reaching the form they now have:

- life   (what Jesus *said and did*),
- oral   (what the apostles *preached*),
- written   (what the evangelists *wrote*).

John refers to these stages, saying:

What we have seen (life stage) . . .
we announce to you (oral stage). . . .
We write this in order (written stage)
that our joy may be complete. 1 JOHN 1:3–4

An unknown poet
writes of the life stage of Jesus:

He never wrote a book. . . .
He never went to college. . . .
He never traveled two hundred miles
from the place where he was born. . . .
While still a young man,
the tide of popular opinion
turned against him.
His friends ran away. . . .
He was nailed to a cross. . . .
When he was dead, he was taken down
and laid in a borrowed grave. . . .
Nineteen wide centuries
have come and gone and he is still
the centerpiece of the human race.

If I could be present at one event
in the life stage of Jesus,
what event would I choose?
Why would I choose this event?

The oral stage of the Gospel begins
on Pentecost and lasts thirty years or so.
Matthew hints at this time-lapse twice,
using the editorial expression
"to this very day" (MATTHEW 27:8, 28:15).

During the oral stage,
parts of the Gospel received the form
they now have in the Bible.

One reason for this is
that Christians undoubtedly used them
at each Lord's Supper (LUKE 24:27).

A part of each Supper consisted
in "remembering" Jesus (LUKE 22:19).
Events linked to the Supper
would be recalled and recited, especially:

- wine miracle at Cana   (JOHN 2:1),
- bread miracle by the sea   (JOHN 6:1),
- Last Supper   (LUKE 22:17),
- Emmaus supper   (LUKE 24:13).

Christians also recalled Jesus' teaching
when they met to discuss moral issues
related to their daily life.
For example, they were criticized for

- ignoring Sabbath laws   (MARK 2:27),
- welcoming sinners   (MARK 2:16),
- paying taxes to Rome   (MARK 12:17).

Suggested reading: Acts 5:40–42

They answered these criticisms
by recalling Jesus' teaching about them.

It is hard for us in an age of print
to appreciate the power and fidelity
of oral communication.
Alex Haley's book *Roots* can help here.

As a boy, Alex used to listen to stories
about his ancestors, such as the story
of Kunta Kinte (*"Kin-tay"*).
Kinte was kidnapped into slavery
while cutting wood near an African river.

Fifty years later, Haley went to Africa
to consult *griots* (*oral* historians)
of his tribal village.
One day while listening to a *griot*
recite family trees, his blood ran cold.
He heard him say, "Omorro Kinte begat
Kunta, who left his village to chop wood
and was never seen again."

It is through a similar *oral* process
that the words and works of Jesus
were remembered and passed on.

*What is one formative episode from
my childhood that few of my friends
or my family know about?*

The final gospel stage is the *written* one.
It begins when the apostles realize
they can't preach the Gospel
to all nations in their lifetime.

Guided by the Holy Spirit,
evangelists (gospel writers), like Luke,
begin to collect, edit, and record
the oral teachings and stories about Jesus.
Luke prefaces his gospel, saying:

*Because I have carefully studied
all these matters from their beginning,
I thought it would be good
to write an orderly account for you.
I do this so that you will know
the full truth about everything
which you have been taught.* LUKE 1:3-4

At times we can see
where the evangelist "stitched" together
a series of memorized events.
Expressions such as "one day" or "once"
are telltale seams where the writer
did this (LUKE 5:1, 12, 17; 6:1).

These "seams" explain
why it is fairly easy to divide the Gospel
into handy "reading packages."
It is because the first Christians
packaged the Gospel this way

to facilitate their use
in two settings or situations, especially—

* public worship and
* instruction of new Christians.

And so the four gospels go through
three stages in their formation:

* life   (what Jesus *said and did*),
* oral   (what the apostles *preached*).
* written   (what the evangelists *wrote*).

An analogy might help to illustrate
these three stages.

The ocean floor is littered
with thousands of seashells.
In time, some of these *floor* shells
wash up onto the beach.
One day an artist is out walking
and sees the *beach* shells.
She picks up the most beautiful ones,
takes them home,
and shapes them into a lovely *vase*.

*Reread the seashell analogy
and decide to which gospel stage
(and why) the following correspond:
the shells on the ocean floor,
the shells that washed onto the beach,
the shells that were formed into a vase.*

Imagine you are a yearbook editor.
In your file are photos
of the key events of the school year.
The question you ask yourself is this:
What approaches might be used
in arranging the photos in the yearbook?
Three possible approaches are

- a historical approach,
- a biographical approach, or
- an invitational approach.

A *historical* approach means you arrange
the photos in the same order in which
they were taken. Thus the yearbook
becomes a *history* of the year.

A *biographical* approach means
you pick a student and follow her or him
through the year. Thus the yearbook
becomes a *biography* of a typical student.

Finally, an *invitational* approach means
you pick the major athletic, academic,
and social events of the year
and arrange them according to themes.
Thus the yearbook becomes an *invitation*
to *relive* these events.

When each of the evangelists sat down
to record the Gospel,
each asked the same question you did:

What approach might be used
in arranging the key events
of Jesus' life and teaching?

Guided by the Holy Spirit,
each chooses the *invitational* approach.

The reason? Each wants to *invite* us
to *relive* the same experiences of Jesus
that the disciples enjoyed.
Each wants to extend to us
the same *invitation* they received:
to *believe* in Jesus
and to have life through him.
John puts it this way in his gospel:

*These [things] have been written
in order that you may believe
that Jesus is the Messiah, the Son of God,
and that through your faith in him
you may have life.* JOHN 20:31

*I imagine that Jesus appears to me,
right now during my prayer.
Addressing me by my first name, he asks,
"What is it that attracts you to me
and to my teaching?
Why have you chosen to follow me,
knowing that it won't be easy?"
What answer do I give to Jesus?*

157

A TV director is planning a program
titled "New York: A Tourist's View."

He decides to present the city
through the eyes of four tourists
as they approach it for the first time:

- by rail   (train),
- by road   (car),
- by water   (boat),
- by air   (plane).

Thus TV viewers will get not one,
but four views of New York.
As a result, their appreciation of the city
will be greatly enriched.

We have something similar
when it comes to Jesus' life and teaching.

Scripture approaches Jesus
through the eyes of four evangelists,
each writing

- at different times,
- in different places, and
- for different audiences.

Experts don't agree totally
on all times, places, and audiences,
but they do agree
that the following are probable:

	TIME (C.E.)	PLACE	AUDIENCE
Mark	–70	Rome	Gentiles
Matthew	70–90	Syria	Jews
Luke	70–90	Greece	Greeks
John	+90	Asia Minor	All people

We may extend our comparison between
the TV producer's approach to New York
and the evangelists' approach to Jesus.

Three approaches to New York
(rail, road, water) are quite similar,
while the fourth (air) is quite different.
Likewise, three gospel approaches to Jesus
(Mark, Matthew, Luke) are quite similar,
while the fourth (John) is quite different.
In fact, Mark, Matthew, and Luke
are so similar that we refer to them
as the *synoptic* gospels (MARK 9:2–5,
MATTHEW 17:1–4, LUKE 9:28–31).

The word *synoptic*—
syn ("together"), *optic* ("seen")—
indicates that when "seen together,"
the similarities are striking.

*Who are three people
who would view me in a similar way?*

Kim's mother describes Kim one way;
Kim's teacher describes her another;
Kim's best friend, a third way;
Kim's volleyball coach, a fourth way.
We have one Kim, but four "portraits."

We have something similar in the gospels.
We have one Jesus, but four portraits.

GOSPEL	PORTRAIT OF JESUS
Mark	*suffering* Messiah
Matthew	*teaching* Messiah
Luke	*compassionate* Messiah
John	*life-giving* Messiah

Mark paints his portrait of Jesus mainly
for persecuted Roman Christians.
He makes it clear
that just as Jesus himself *suffered*,
so they can expect to suffer also.

Matthew paints his portrait mainly
for Christians of Jewish background.
He stresses that Jesus' *teaching*
dovetails with the teaching of Moses
and the Old Testament prophets.
Jesus did not come to abolish the law,
but to fulfill it (MATTHEW 5:17).

Luke paints his portrait mainly
for Greek Gentiles (non-Jews).

Many were among society's outcasts.
He stresses Jesus' *compassion*
for second-class citizens of his day.
For example, Luke documents
Jesus' special concern for women
with data found in no other gospel
(LUKE 7:11–17, 8:1–3, 15:8–10, 18:1–8).

Finally, *John* paints his portrait
for Christians of all walks of life.
Therefore, John stresses
the *life-giving* dimension of Jesus.
Jesus has come
to enrich life in this world and
to ensure life in the world to come.

"I have come . . .
that you might have life—
life in all its fullness." JOHN 10:10

Since John wrote at a later time
than the others, his portrait reflects
a more seasoned view of Jesus.

And so the gospels present us
with not just one portrait of Jesus,
but four.

Which of the four portraits do I
find most relevant for today? Why?

Fire swept through Rome in 64 C.E.
Rumor said Emperor Nero set the fire
to have an excuse to build a new city
and name it for himself.
To shift suspicion from himself,
Nero blamed Christians for the fire
and persecuted them brutally.
The ancient historian Tacitus says:

They were put on crosses and,
at nighttime, burned as torches
to light up the darkness.

Tradition says Mark came to Rome
with Peter and wrote, mainly,
for Roman Christians, which explains
his focus on Jesus' suffering.

Tradition also says that Mark
is the young man who guided the apostles
to the Last Supper room (MARK 14:12–16).
Some think it belonged to Mark's mother
and served later as a meeting place
for early Christians (ACTS 12:12).

After the meal,
Mark may have followed
the apostles and Jesus to Gethsemane,
narrowly escaping arrest (MARK 14:51).

Mark begins his gospel, saying:

This is the Good News
about Jesus Christ, the Son of God.

This provides the broad two-part outline
that Mark follows in his gospel:

- part 1:   Jesus is the Christ
- part 2:   Jesus is the Son of God

The first part of Mark's gospel
focuses on Jesus
as "the Christ" ("the Messiah").
It ends with Peter saying to Jesus,
"You are the Messiah" (MARK 8:29).

The second part of Mark's gospel
focuses on Jesus as the "Son of God."
It ends with a Roman soldier saying at
Jesus' crucifixion, "This man
was really the Son of God" (MARK 15:39).

An interesting literary device
that Mark uses is to ask a question
and not answer it.

Thus when Jesus calms the sea,
his disciples ask in astonishment,
"Who is this man?" (MARK 4:41).

How do I answer the question
posed by the disciples?

Tradition identifies Matthew
as the tax collector whom Jesus called
to be one of "the Twelve" (MATTHEW 9:9).

In composing his gospel,
Matthew seems to have had access
to Mark's gospel (or Mark's source).
Occasionally the two gospels match
word for word (MARK 9:2–3, MATTHEW 17:1–13).
But Matthew also includes material
not found in Mark (MATTHEW 1–2).
Matthew's gospel divides into

- a prologue   (Jesus' early years),
- a body   (Jesus' kingdom teaching),
- an epilogue   (Jesus' death and rising).

Matthew's *prologue* and *epilogue*
are subtly matched.
For example, Matthew's quotation
from Isaiah, "God is with us" (MATTHEW 1:23),
is matched by a quotation from Jesus,
"I am with you always" (MATTHEW 28:30).

The *body* of Matthew's gospel
divides into "five instructions."
The "five instructions of Jesus"
form a symbolic parallel to
the "five books of Moses" (Jewish Torah).
Thus Jesus' instructions are portrayed
as a kind of *Christian Torah*.

Each instruction opens with a narrative
that sets the stage for the instruction.
All "five instructions"
relate to the Kingdom of God:

- its demands   (5:1–7:28),
- its proclamation   (10:5–11:1),
- its development   (13:1–53),
- its structure   (8:1–19:1),
- its completion   (23:1–26:1).

Each of the "five instructions" ends
with a similarly worded formula:
"When Jesus finished his teaching"
(MATTHEW 7:28, 11:1, 13:53, 19:1, 26:1).

Writing mainly for Jewish Christians,
Matthew is primarily concerned with
showing how Jesus and his teaching
fulfill Jewish prophecy and teaching.
Thus Matthew takes pains to match
Jesus' life with biblical prophecies
(MATTHEW 1:23; 2:6, 15, 18, 23).

And so Matthew's portrait of Jesus
is that of the "teaching Messiah."
Jesus fulfills Jewish hopes and dreams.

*What strikes me most about the way
Matthew structures his gospel and
presents the teaching of Jesus?*

It surprises some people to learn
that Luke and Paul traveled together.
Paul refers to this, writing:

- "Luke, our dear doctor" (COLOSSIANS 4:14);
- "Luke is with me" (2 TIMOTHY 4:11);
- "Luke sends you greetings" (PHILEMON 24).

Likewise, Luke, who wrote
both his gospel and Acts (ACTS 1:1),
alludes to Paul.
He does this subtly, shifting from
"he" (Paul) to "we" (Luke and Paul)
(ACTS 16:10–17, 20:5–21:18, 27:1–28:16).

Luke structures his gospel
according to this fivefold outline:

- ministry prologue (1:5–4:13),
- Galilean ministry (4:14–9:50),
- journey to Jerusalem (9:51–19:27),
- Jerusalem ministry (19:28–21:38),
- ministry epilogue (22:1–22:53).

Luke explains Jewish customs
(LUKE 22:1, 23:56) and the location
of Jewish towns (LUKE 4:31, 23:51, 24:13).
This orients his Gentile, Greek readers.

Luke stresses Jesus' concern
for society's oppressed citizens,
especially the poor and the powerless:

"Happy are you poor;
the Kingdom of God is yours!
Happy are you who are hungry now;
you will be filled!
Happy are you who weep now;
you will laugh!" LUKE 6:20–21

Luke's stress
on Jesus' concern for the oppressed
inspired W. D. Davies to write:

The Jesus of Luke
might well have uttered the words
written on the Statue of Liberty
in New York Harbor:

"Give me your tired, your poor,
your huddled masses
yearning to breathe free. . . .
Send these, the homeless,
the tempest-tost to me."

And so Luke portrays Jesus fulfilling

- Jewish dreams and
- Gentile dreams.

What was it that struck me most
about Luke the evangelist?
About Luke the human being?

Tradition says John was Zebedee's son,
James's brother (LUKE 5:10), and
the disciple "whom Jesus loved."
John enjoys a privileged presence

- at the Last Supper (JOHN 13:23),
- under the cross (JOHN 19:26),
- at the tomb (JOHN 20:2),
- on the seashore (JOHN 21:7).

John begins his gospel with a prologue
that previews his approach to Jesus,
which is quite different from that
of the other three evangelists. He writes:

In the beginning,
the Word already existed. . . .
The Word was the source of life,
and this life brought light to people.
The light shines in the darkness, and
the darkness has never put it out. JOHN 1:1, 4–5

One reason for John's different approach
is that he writes at a later date and
addresses a maturer Christian audience.

Some of the ways John's gospel differs
from the other gospels are the following:
First, he rarely uses the story format.
When he does, he is more interested
in the story's symbolism:

- *water*   woman at well (JOHN 4:14),
- *bread*   crowd feeding (JOHN 6:1–51),
- *blindness*   sightless man (JOHN 9:39).

Second, John has Jesus identify himself
with God's sacred name "I am" (EXODUS 3:14).
Jesus says: "I am

- the bread of life"   (JOHN 6:35),
- the light of the world"   (JOHN 8:12),
- the good shepherd"   (JOHN 10:11).

Third, John identifies Jesus, almost
immediately, as the Messiah (JOHN 1:41).

Fourth, John's gospel
reflects a sacramental dimension:

- Baptism   (JOHN 3:1–6),
- Eucharist   (JOHN 6:53),
- Reconciliation   (JOHN 20:23).

Finally, John substitutes "eternal life"
in place of the "Kingdom of God."

In brief, John's portrait of Jesus is that
of the "life-giving" Messiah (JOHN 10:10).

*What are my thoughts
as I reread the excerpt from the prologue
of John's gospel?*

169

The word *gospel* is a translation
of the Greek word *evangelion*.
Concretely, *gospel* means "good news."

The Old Testament
uses this word a number of times.
For example, Isaiah says:

Proclaim the good news! . . .
Call out with a loud voice, Zion;
announce the good news!
Speak out and do not be afraid.
Tell the towns of Judah
that their God is coming! ISAIAH 40:9

The word *gospel* is used
the same way in the New Testament.
For example, Jesus says:

"The Kingdom of God is near!
Turn away from your sins and believe
the Good News [Gospel]." MARK 1:15

Some New Testament translations
capitalize *Gospel (Good News)* to stress
that it is the *definitive* "Good News."

Not until the second century is
the plural form of the word *gospel* used.
Then Christian writers
begin speaking of "the four gospels."
The title they give the individual gospels

is "The Gospel according to Matthew"
(Mark, Luke, or John).
The phrase *according to* reminds us
that each gospel
was passed on orally for a long time.
Therefore each gospel is
the *written record* of an *oral tradition,*
for example, the preaching of Matthew.

It is important to keep this in mind,
because the actual recording
of "The Gospel *according to* Matthew"
need not have been done
by the apostle Matthew himself.
A student of his could have done it.

The important thing is not
who actually committed it to writing.
The important thing is
that it is the *inspired record*
of an *oral tradition* about Jesus,
as preached by the apostle Matthew.

A Brahman priest told a missionary,
"If you Christians in India, in Britain,
or in America were like your Bible,
you would conquer India in five years."
What, especially, keeps my own life
from being "like my Bible"?

171

Darrel Doré was trapped inside an oil rig
that had just sunk in the Gulf of Mexico.
As its platform filled with water,
a huge air bubble formed in one corner.
Darrel thrust his head inside it.

There he shivered and prayed for hours.
When he was about to give up, a tiny "star
of light" appeared in the watery darkness.
It was the light of a diver's helmet.

Doré's rescue at sea is a beautiful image
of humanity's rescue from sin.
Just when humanity was about to give up,
a tiny "star of light" appeared
in the darkness of the Bethlehem sky:

*Shepherds . . . were spending the night
in the fields, taking care of their flocks.
An angel of the Lord appeared . . .
[saying], "This very day in David's town
your Savior was born—Christ the Lord! . . .
You will find a baby wrapped in cloths
and lying in a manger."* LUKE 2:8–12

This passage points to Jesus' *identity*,
mission, and future *lifestyle*. How so?

Luke says that shepherds were
"in the fields, taking care of their flocks."
Normally, shepherds crowded their sheep
into pens for the night. The one season

they didn't do this was lambing season
(lest new lambs be trampled to death).

Luke's account suggests that
Jesus was born during lambing season.
Further, lambs born around Bethlehem
were destined for sacrifice in the Temple
in nearby Jerusalem.

And so Jesus' birth
during lambing season and *at Bethlehem*
points to Jesus' identity and *mission*:
He is the "Lamb of God,"
destined for "sacrifice" in Jerusalem.

Finally, the passage points to
the future *lifestyle* that Jesus will adopt.
Luke says "an angle of the Lord"
tells the shepherds
they will find the baby "lying in a manger."

This suggests that the adult Jesus
will not have a palace and identify himself
with the rich and the powerful.
Rather, he will have no place at all
and identify himself
with the poor and the powerless (LUKE 9:58).

*What strikes or challenges me most
about these circumstances of Jesus' birth?*

173

In his book *Roots*, Alex Haley tells how
his African ancestors named a child.
Eight days after the child's birth,
the father whispers its name in its ear.
Africans believe the child
should be the first to know its name.

The same night, under the night sky,
the father completes the "naming" rite.
Pointing to the star-filled sky,
the father says to the child, "Behold—
the only thing greater than yourself."

Jewish parents also had special rites
for naming a child and
introducing it into the world (LUKE 2:21–24).
The rite took place in the Temple
and involved circumcision, presentation,
and purification of the mother
(GENESIS 17:10, EXODUS 13, LEVITICUS 12).

- *Circumcision* initiates the child
  into the community of God's people.
- *Presentation* consecrates it to God
  in gratitude for saving Israel's firstborn
  from the final plague in Egypt.
- *Purification* welcomes the mother
  back into full participation
  in the worshiping community.

When Joseph and Mary bring Jesus
to the Temple for these rites,

two elderly Jews, Simeon and Anna,
happen to be there at the time.
Both had prayed all their lives to see
the promised Messiah before they died.
Seeing Jesus, Simeon cradles him
in his arms, gives thanks, and says:

"Lord, you have kept your promise. . . .
With my own eyes
I have seen your salvation . . . :
A light to reveal your will
to the Gentiles and
bring glory to your people Israel." . . .

[Simeon says to Mary,] "This child . . .
will be a sign from God which
many people will speak against. . . .
And sorrow, like a sharp sword,
will break your own heart."

[Similarly, Anna] gave thanks to God
and spoke about the child
to all who were waiting for God
to set Jerusalem free.

LUKE 2:29-30, 32, 34-35, 38

What are some of my thoughts
as I imagine myself to be Mary,
listening to Simeon's prophecy,
especially about the sharp sword?

175

Sometime after Jesus' birth,
magi from the East arrived in Jerusalem.

MAGI   *Where is the baby born to be*
            the king of the Jews?
            We saw his star
            when it came up in the east. . . .

NARRATOR   *When King Herod*
            heard about this,
            he was very upset. . . .

HEROD   *[to his advisors] Where*
            will the Messiah be born? . . .

ADVISORS   *Bethlehem in Judea.* . . . , *For this*
            is what the prophet wrote:
            "Bethlehem . . . , *from you*
            will come a leader who will
            guide my people Israel."

NARRATOR   *And so [the visitors] left.* . . .
            When they saw the child . . .
            they [presented him
            with] gifts of gold, frankincense,
            and myrrh.   MATTHEW 2:2–6, 9, 11

This story—recorded some seventy years
after Jesus' birth—is like a tapestry,
woven from three threads:

• history   (remembered events),
• prophecy   (biblical prophecies),
• inspiration   (divine guidance).

History says the magi were from Persia. They were not kings but advisors to kings in matters of science and religion.

Prophecy in the Old Testament foretells that the Messiah will

- be born in Bethlehem (MICAH 5:2),
- shine like a bright star (NUMBERS 24:17),
- receive royal gifts (PSALM 72:10–11).

Inspiration from the Holy Spirit guided Matthew to compose the story in a way that the gifts of the magi point, symbolically, to Jesus' identity.

- *Gold* was the "king of metals" and points to Jesus' *kingship*.
- *Frankincense* was used in worship and points to Jesus' *divinity*.
- *Myrrh* was used in Jewish burials and points to Jesus' *humanity*.

Finally, the reactions of King Herod and the magi story preview two things:

—Many Jews will reject him;
—many Gentiles will welcome him.

What aspect of the magi story impresses me most? Why this?

The boyhood life of Jesus probably
differed little, externally, from the lives
of other Jewish boys his age.
No doubt he climbed hills with friends,
tracked foxes (LUKE 9:58),
and chatted with shepherds (JOHN 10:1–10).

The Talmud (a Jewish religious manual)
says of a Jewish boy:

*At five he must begin sacred studies;
at ten he must set himself
to learning the tradition;
at thirteen he must know the whole law
of Yahweh and live it faithfully.*

In modern times, the rite of *Bar Mitzvah*
("Son of the Law") celebrates
a boy's entry into young adulthood.
This explains why the young Jesus
goes to Jerusalem with adult Jews
from Nazareth to celebrate the Passover.
It marks his entry into young adulthood.

After the Passover, the throng of pilgrims
depart from Jerusalem to return home.
When Mary and Joseph find Jesus missing,
they go in search of him.

NARRATOR *They found him in the Temple,
sitting with the Jewish
teachers, listening to them*

*and asking questions. All who
heard him were amazed. . . .*

MARY   *Son, why have you done this
to us? Your father and I
have been terribly worried
trying to find you.*

JESUS   *Why did you have to look for me?
Didn't you know that I had to be
in my Father's house?*

NARRATOR *But they did not understand
his answer. So Jesus went
back with them to Nazareth,
where he was obedient. . . .
His mother treasured all
these things in her heart.*

LUKE 2:46–51

Jesus' response to Mary
suggests that amid the ordinariness
of daily life in Nazareth,
something beautiful has been taking place
within the mind and heart of Jesus.

His awareness of himself and
of his earthly mission is taking shape.
Jesus is maturing "in body and
in wisdom, gaining favor
with God and people" (LUKE 2:52).

*What might Jesus say if I asked him
why he answered his mother as he did?*

179

Linda had one foot in the shower and
one out. "This is a good picture of my life,"
she thought. "I want to choose God,
but I keep one foot in and one foot out."
After a pause, she said, "I choose God!"
Then she stepped into the shower.
"That was a real baptism!" she said later.

John the Baptist invited people to make
a similar decision and be baptized.
One day he was shocked to see Jesus
step into the water to be baptized.

[Suddenly] heaven was opened,
and the Holy Spirit came down upon him
in bodily form like a dove.
And a voice came from heaven,
"You are my own dear Son." LUKE 3:21–22

The key to understanding this passage is
its three images: *heaven opening*, the
dove descending, and the *voice speaking*.

Jews pictured the universe
as three worlds stacked like pancakes.

God resided in the top world (heaven);
the people, in the middle world (earth); and
the dead, in the bottom world (sheol).
After Adam's sin,
the middle world grew more and more evil.

Jews begged God to "tear the sky open and
come down," and correct things (PSALM 144:5).
The image of *heaven opening* signals
that God is answering their prayers.
A *new era* is dawning.

The image of the *dove descending* recalls
God's power descending upon the waters
before the creation of the world.
Rabbis compared God's power to a dove.
The image of the dove descending signals
the dawn of a new creation. God is
fulfilling the promise to Isaiah: "The LORD
says, 'I am making a new earth' " (ISAIAH 65:17).

Finally, the image of the *voice speaking*
from heaven identifies Jesus
as the *new Adam* of the *new creation.*
"The first Adam . . . came from earth,
the second Adam came from heaven"
(1 CORINTHIANS 15:47).

And so the three baptismal images signal:

* a new era   (heaven opening),
* a new creation   (dove descending),
* a new Adam   (voice speaking).

*How do I experience the presence
of the "two Adams" in myself?*

Doug Alderson left for a summer's hike
down the Appalachian Trail. He said:

I had just graduated from high school.
I had many questions.
My goals in life?
My future? Was there a God? . . .
My hike was a search to find myself.

Five months later
he returned home a changed person.
Even his dog eyed him suspiciously,
as if to say, "Where have you been?
You look different." Doug was different.
He had found what he was searching for.

Doug Alderson belongs
to that long line of people in history
who have gone off alone for a time
to commune with God and themselves.

Moses did it; the prophets did it;
John the Baptist did it.
And so it comes as no surprise
to learn that Jesus did it also.

NARRATOR   *After spending forty days*
and nights without food,
Jesus was hungry. . . .

DEVIL   *If you are God's Son, order*
these stones to turn into bread.

JESUS	*The scripture says, "Human beings* *cannot live on bread alone,* *but need every word* *that God speaks." . . .*
DEVIL	*If you are God's Son, throw* *yourself [from the Temple]. . . .* *Scripture says, ". . . angels . . .* *will hold you up with their hands. . . ."*
JESUS	*Scripture also says, "Do not* *put the Lord . . . to the test."*
NARRATOR	*Then the Devil . . . showed him* *all the kingdoms of the world* *in all their greatness.*
DEVIL	*All this I will give you, if you* *kneel down and worship me.*
JESUS	*Go away, Satan! The scripture* *says, "Worship the Lord . . .* *and serve only him!"* MATTHEW 4:2–10

This desert encounter with the Tempter
gives us an insight into the answers
to three big questions about Jesus:

- Who is he?
- What has he come to do?
- How will he do it?

How does the desert encounter
point to Jesus' identity, mission, and lifestyle?

Jesus' victory over the Tempter suggests
answers to these three big questions
about Jesus:

- Who is he?   his identity
- What has he come to do?   his mission
- How will he do it?   his lifestyle

First, his victory suggests his identity.
Jesus is not just *a* "son of man" (human)
but also *the* "Son of God" (divine).

Second, his victory suggests his mission.
After God created Adam,
the Tempter induced Adam to sin.
That sin brought *death to all* (ROMANS 5:12).

Now Satan repeats the process.
He tempts Jesus, the *new* Adam.
Jesus stands firm; his victory restores
life to all. Paul writes:

As all people die
because of their union with Adam, ...
all will be raised to life
because of their union with Christ.
                   1 CORINTHIANS 15:22

Finally, Jesus' victory over Satan
suggests the lifestyle he will follow.

His refusal
to *turn bread to stone* suggests that

he will not use his powers
to avoid suffering.
Rather, he will suffer, just as we do.

His refusal to *leap off the Temple
and be rescued by angels* suggests that
he has come
not to be served by other people,
but to serve them (MARK 10:45).

Finally, his refusal to *bow to Satan*,
in exchange for control of the world,
suggests that
he will not compromise with evil.
Sin will never be an option for him.

And so the encounter with the Tempter
clarifies three things about Jesus:

- his *identity:*   he is human and divine;
- his *mission:*   he gives life to all;
- his *lifestyle:*   he suffers, serves, is sinless.

*How do I explain
these words of Peter Taylor Forsyth
and apply them to Jesus and to my life?
"Unless there is within us
that which is above us,
we shall soon yield to
that which is about us."*

185

Jesus left the desert, "and the power
of the Holy Spirit with with him" (LUKE 4:14).
He took the road north to Galilee and
went to the lakeside town of Capernaum.
There he preached that the inauguration
of God's Kingdom on earth was at hand.

His words created enormous excitement.
People came from nearby towns and
invited him to preach in their synagogues.
It was during this preaching tour that
Jesus stopped at Nazareth, his hometown.

On the Sabbath
he went as usual to the synagogue. . . .
He unrolled the scroll and
found the place where it is written,

"The Spirit of the Lord is upon me,
because he has chosen me. . . .
The time has come
when the Lord will save his people." . . .
[Jesus ended, saying,] "This passage
of scripture has come true today,
as you heard it being read." LUKE 4:16–19, 21

The reaction of the people swung
like a pendulum from one of marveling
at his eloquence to one of challenging
what he had just said.
For centuries, Jews had dreamed about

the Messiah and prayed for his coming.
Now someone they had watched grow up
stood before them and claimed
that he was that "promised one."

Then Jesus challenged them for rejecting
him merely because of where he grew up.

When the people . . .
heard this, they were filled with anger.
They rose up, dragged Jesus out of town,
and took him to the top of the hill
on which their town was built.
They meant to throw him over the cliff,
but he walked through the middle of
the crowd and went his way. LUKE 4:28–30

This frightening episode shocks us.
It takes us back to Simeon's prophecy
that Jesus "will be a sign from God
which many people will speak against."

The rejection of Jesus in his hometown
makes clear what lays ahead for him:
opposition from those he loves
and, eventually, death at their hands.

What are my thoughts as I imagine
myself to be Mary, watching her son
being rejected by those they both loved?

Jesus shook the dust of Nazareth
from his feet and returned to Capernaum.
On the Sabbath he went to the synagogue
and preached to the people.

They were all amazed at the way he taught,
because he spoke with authority.

In the synagogue was a man who had
the spirit of an evil demon in him. . . .
Jesus ordered the spirit, . . .
"Come out of the man!"
The demon . . . went out of him. . . .
The people were all amazed. . . .
And the report about Jesus spread. . . .

All who had friends who were sick . . .
brought them to Jesus;
he . . . healed them all. LUKE 4:32–33, 35–37, 40

The gospels use three Greek words
to describe Jesus' miracles:
teras, dynamis, and *semion.*

- *Teras* means "marvel."
  It stresses that Jesus' miracles
  amazed people.
- *Dynamis* means "power."
  We get our word *dynamite* from it.
  It stresses that Jesus' miracles
  showed him possessed of
  a remarkable godlike power.

- *Semion* means "sign."
  It stresses that Jesus' miracles
  made people ask one another,
  "What does this mean?"

We might compare Jesus' miracles
to a flashing red light.
The important thing isn't the light,
but what it signifies, what it means.
The same is true of Jesus' miracles.

This raises the key question:
What was Jesus trying to say
to the people through his miracles?

They have a twofold meaning. They act as

- proclamations and
- invitations.

They *proclaim* Jesus is the Messiah,
who is inaugurating God's Kingdom.
They *invite* people to open their hearts
to Jesus and God's Kingdom.

We will look more closely
at these two points in the days ahead.

*Practically speaking, how do I open
my heart to God's Kingdom and let God
reign as King over it?*

189

The movie *The Exorcist* is based on a real
exorcism of a fourteen-year-old boy
from Mount Rainier, Maryland.
Newsweek writes:

The boy's bed would suddenly move about.
At night, he could hardly sleep. . . .
He was admitted
to Georgetown University Hospital.
While strapped in his bed,
long red scratches appeared on his body.
[The boy underwent an exorcism
and is now completely normal.]

Jesus also does successful exorcisms.
This amazes people, who exclaim,
"What is this?. . .
Evil spirits . . . obey him!" (MARK 1:27).

The people's question introduces us
to the three ways that miracles *proclaim*
Jesus to be the promised Messiah,
who is inaugurating God's Kingdom.

The *first way* is by showing evil spirits
obeying Jesus' commands. Jesus said,
"[This] proves that the Kingdom of God
has . . . come upon you" (LUKE 11:20).

The *second way* miracles proclaim
Jesus is the Messiah is by showing
his power over *sin*, *sickness*, and *death*.

These three evils entered the world
through Adam's sin.

By *forgiving* sin, *healing* sickness,
and *raising* the dead, Jesus shows
that Satan's kingdom is dying and
God's Kingdom is being born.

The *third way* miracles *proclaim*
Jesus to be the Messiah
is by fulfilling the prophecies.

Isaiah foretold that certain signs
would announce the Messiah's coming:
"The blind will . . . see, and the deaf
will hear. The lame will leap" (ISAIAH 35:5–6).
This is what Jesus' miracles do.

And so miracles *proclaim* Jesus is the
Messiah, who is inaugurating God's Kingdom,
 in three ways. They show him

- expelling demons,
- destroying sin, sickness, and death, and
- fulfilling biblical prophecy.

How do I answer Joseph Lewis, who said,
"If I had the power the New Testament
says that Jesus had, I would not cure
one person of blindness.
I would make blindness impossible"?

Bruce Marshall wrote a novel
called *Father Malachy's Miracle*.
It centers around a priest in Scotland,
who gets the idea of praying for a miracle
so obvious that no one can deny it.
He prays that the town's sinful nightclub
be lifted up and carried
to a desolate island off the town's coast.

The miracle happens in view of everyone.
But it doesn't convert anyone.
Instead, the nightclub's owners
turn Father Malachy's miracle
into a huge, profitable publicity stunt.

The story ends with Malachy realizing
that you can't *compel* belief;
you can only *invite* it.

This brings us
to the second purpose of Jesus' miracles.
Besides *proclaiming* God's Kingdom,
they *invite* us to open our hearts to it.
How do they do this?

The healings of the blind and the deaf
and the raising of the dead—
these are not permanent changes.

The eyes of the blind will dim again;
the ears of the deaf will close again;
and people raised to life will die again.

What, then, is the "eternal value"
of these miracles?
What is their abiding significance?

They are *invitations* to the people
of Jesus' day—and of our own day.

The healing of the *blind* invites us
to open our eyes to what Jesus does.
The healing of the *deaf* invites us
to open our ears to what Jesus says.
The raising of the *dead* invites us
to open our hearts to the Kingdom
and be reborn, spiritually.

And so Jesus' miracles
are *signs* to all who experience them:

- They *proclaim*
  that Jesus is the promised Messiah,
  who is inaugurating God's Kingdom;
- they *invite* us
  to open our hearts to God's Kingdom
  and let God in to rule as King over us.

Imagine that a dead parent or relative
returned from the dead and said,
"Life on the other side is just as
Jesus said it was."
How would this affect my faith? Why?

People in gospel times
responded to Jesus' miracles
in different ways.

Many believed and opened their hearts
to God's Kingdom (JOHN 4:53).
Others refused to believe and closed
their eyes to Jesus' miracles (JOHN 9:18).
Still others acknowledged Jesus' miracles
but said Satan empowered him
to perform them (LUKE 11:15).

Today, people still respond
in different ways to Jesus' miracles.
Some say Jesus only cured people
of epilepsy, which ancients interpreted
as being a demon.
Still others say Jesus only raised people
from deep comas but not from death.

Jesus told a parable to illustrate
the four main ways that people
can respond to his works—and his words.

A farmer sowed seed in his field.
(Ancients sowed seed atop the soil
and then plowed it under.)

Some seed fell on a path by the field.
Birds snatched it up and ate it instantly.
Some fell on the thin layer of soil
that covered flat rocks in the field.

It sprouted quickly but died
when the sun baked the soil dry.
Some blew into thornbushes
that formed a fence around the field
to keep wild animals out.
This seed sprouted but got choked quickly.
Finally, some seed fell on good soil
and bore abundant fruit. Jesus explained:

*"The seeds that fell along the path
stand for those who hear; but the Devil
comes and takes the message away. . . ."*

*"The seeds that fell on rocky ground
stand for those who hear the message
and receive it gladly. . . . But when the
time of testing comes, they fall away.*

*"The seeds that fell among thorn bushes
stand for those who hear; but the worries
and riches and pleasures of this life . . .
choke them, and their fruit never ripens.*

*"The seeds that fell in good soil
stand for those who hear the message
and . . . bear fruit."* LUKE 8:12–15

*Which seed am I most like
when it comes to my response to Jesus'
words and work—the seed that fell
on the path? Rock? Thorns? Soil? Why?*

Four modern stories illustrate
the four responses to Jesus' miracles.
The first concerns a girl who wrote:

*When we were discussing Jesus' parable
about the farmer planting seeds,
I got the feeling he was talking to me.
Last year I talked with my counselor.
She helped me see a lot of things,
and I made several resolutions. . . .
Then it hit me: I hadn't followed up
on a single one of them.*

The second story concerns a man
who describes an important event
that took place in his youth.
One Sunday night he knelt down
and committed his life to Jesus.
The next day he wrote:

*Jesus has come into my house.
He has cleansed it and now rules it. . . .
I really have felt an immense new joy. . . .
It is the joy
of being at peace with the world and
being in touch with God.
I never really knew God before.*

JOHN R. STOTT

The third story concerns
British TV celebrity Kenneth Clark.

He describes a "spiritual experience"
that moved him to consider
making major changes in his life.
But he ended up doing nothing, saying:

I think I was right:
I was too deeply embedded in the world
to change course.
But that I had "felt the finger of God,"
I was quite sure.

The final story concerns two brothers,
Clarence and Robert.
Both had committed their lives to Jesus.
Clarence became a civil rights activist;
Robert, a lawyer with political dreams.
One day Clarence asked Robert
for legal help. Robert refused,
saying it could hurt his political future.
When Clarence asked him about
his commitment to Jesus, Robert said,
"I do follow Jesus, but not to the cross.
I'm not going to get crucified as he was."
Clarence replied, "You're not a follower
of Jesus; you're only one of his fans."

How do these stories illustrate
the following in Jesus' parable:
the grain that fell on the path?
On rock? Among thorns? On good soil?

A girl reported having visions of Mary
outside Lourdes, France, in 1858.
At once, crippled and sick people
began to visit the site and were healed.

Today the Medical Bureau of Lourdes
has on file over 1,200 confirmed healings.
Each was examined by a commission
of twenty physicians and surgeons
before being accepted as a healing.

In the 1930s a New York surgeon and
Nobel prize winner, Dr. Alexis Carrel,
went to Lourdes to investigate its claims.

While en route by train, he was called
several times to attend to a sick girl,
who was on her way to Lourdes also.
He told a friend, "If a case such as hers
were cured, it would indeed be a miracle.
I would never doubt again."

Dr. Carrel accompanied her to the shrine.
He described his experience
in *The Voyage to Lourdes*.
For professional reasons,
he changed all names of those involved
and called himself Lerrac.

Lerrac felt himself turning pale.
The blanket which covered

*Marie Ferrand's distended abdomen
was gradually flattening out. . . .
"How do you feel?" he asked her. . . .
"I feel I am cured."*

Later he and two other doctors
examined her and pronounced her cured.
That night Lerrac went for a long walk,
ending up in a church. He prayed:

*"I am still blind. . . . I still doubt. . . .
Beneath the deep, harsh warnings
of my intellectual pride
a smothered dream persists. . . .
It is the dream of believing. . . ."*

*Back at his hotel . . . he sat down
to write his observations. . . .
By now it was three o'clock. . . .
A new coolness
penetrated the open window.
He felt the serenity of nature
enter his soul with a gentle calm. . . .
All intellectual doubts had vanished.*

*What does Barbara Ward have in mind
when she says, "Faith will not
be restored to the West because people
believe it to be useful. It will return
only when they find that it is true"?*

During a Super Bowl interview,
former pro star Reggie Williams revealed
that as a child he had been partially deaf.
Teachers dismissed him as "slow."

When Reggie got to the third grade,
a teacher named Miss Chapman took an
interest in him and diagnosed his problem.
Reggie graduated from high school
near the top of his class. He said,
"If Miss Chapman hadn't helped me,
I don't know where I'd be today."

The help Miss Chapman gave Reggie
spotlights the "heart" of Jesus' teaching.
Jesus made love the *sign* and the *power*
of God's Kingdom.

As *sign*, love identifies the presence
of God's Kingdom on earth.
Jesus told his disciples, "If you have love
for one another, then everyone will know
that you are my disciples" (JOHN 13:35).

As *power*, love spreads God's Kingdom
on earth. Jesus told his disciples,
"I love you just as the Father loves me. . . .
Love one another,
just as I love you" (JOHN 15:9, 12).

How does love *spread* God's Kingdom?
An example will demonstrate.

A man was boarding a crowded bus.
Suddenly someone shoved ahead of him,
almost knocking him to the pavement.
He said in *mock* sincerity,
"Forgive me! I didn't mean to block your way!"
The other person was taken aback
and said with *true* sincerity,
"I'm sorry! That was really rude of me."

Now the man was taken aback.
The offending person had responded
to his mock display of love as if it
were real, and was transformed by it.

Later, when the man had a chance
to reflect on what had happened,
he suddenly saw why love is so *powerful*
and how it *spreads* God's Kingdom.
It destroys the "chain reaction of evil"
unleashed by Adam's sin and replaces it
with a "chain reaction of good."

To what extent do I try
to live by these beautiful words
of the poet Edwin Markham:
"He drew a circle that shut me out—
Heretic, rebel, a thing to flout.
But love and I had the wit to win.
We drew a circle that took him in"?

Someone asked, "Who is my neighbor?"
Jesus answered:

"A man . . . was going . . . to Jericho
when robbers attacked him, . . .
leaving him half dead.
It so happened that a priest
was going down that road. . . .
When he saw the man,
he walked on by on the other side.
In the same way a Levite . . .
walked on by on the other side.
But a Samaritan . . . came upon the man,
and when he saw him,
his heart was filled with pity. . . .
He . . . took him to an inn,
where he took care of him. LUKE 10:30–34

Jesus shocked his listeners by making
the hero of his story a Samaritan.

Jews shunned Samaritans as "no-goods"
who had compromised their faith.
Jews banned them from the Temple,
refused their contributions, and would
not accept their testimony in court.

But Jesus had a good reason for making
the Samaritan the hero of his parable.
He was dramatizing
an important truth about God's Kingdom.

In the Kingdom of God,
there are no longer people
who are or who are not neighbors.
There are no more neighbors at all.
There are only brothers and sisters.
And where there are only brother and
sisters, love never walks on by.
It stops to help, especially those in need.

The parable of the Good Samaritan
turned the world of Jesus' listeners
upside down. It made them rethink
their traditional attitudes
toward people, especially enemies.
Years later, Paul expressed it this way:

By his death on the cross
Christ destroyed their enmity; . . .
he united both races into one body
and brought them back to God. . . .
It is through Christ that all of us,
Jews and Gentiles, are able to come
in the one Spirit into the presence
of the Father. EPHESIANS 2:16, 18

"Our lives no longer belong to us alone;
they belong to all
who need us desperately." ELIE WIESEL
Do I know of such a person? Who?

Jesus' parable of the Good Samaritan
prepares the people
for his most *revolutionary* teaching.
It comes in the Sermon on the Mount.
Jesus says to the people:

"Happy are the pure in heart;
they will see God!
Happy are those who work for peace;
God will call them his children! . . .

"You have heard that it was said,
'Love your friends, hate your enemies.'
But now I tell you: love your enemies
and pray for those who persecute you,
so that you may become the children
of your Father in heaven. . . .
Be perfect—just as your Father
in heaven is perfect." MATTHEW 5:8–9, 43–45, 48

The people sit stunned.
Jesus is telling them that no one—
not even their enemies—
should fall outside the boundary of love.

A modern example
of what Jesus is teaching them
is reported in *Newsweek* magazine:

When Gerald Lipke awakened . . .
the first thing he did was turn on
the radio. Jerry, who is 11,

likes to listen to the news
while he is dressing for school.
That morning the news was bad:
United Air Lines Flight 629
with 44 persons aboard had exploded
and crashed the night before.

It turned out that someone
had placed a bomb on flight 629.
Jerry's parents were on the flight.

Later the students of Jerry's school
asked their pastor for a prayer service.
The pastor checked with Jerry,
who said he would like that very much.
Then Jerry added,
"Could we also say a prayer for the man
who killed my mother and father?"

That story dramatizes and summarizes
Jesus' teaching about love. It is

• the *sign* of God's Kingdom and
• the *power* that "re-creates" our world.

How well do I understand and practice
these words of Thomas Merton:
"Pure love and prayer
are learned in the hour
when prayer has become impossible
and your heart has turned to stone"?

Some religious leaders were grumbling
about Jesus, saying:

"This man welcomes outcasts
and even eats with them!"
So Jesus told them this parable. . . .
"There was once a man who had two sons.
The younger one [took his inheritance,
left home, spent all, and returned broke.]
He was still a long way from home
when his father saw him, . . .
ran [to meet him], . . . and kissed him. . . .
[The father told his servants,]
"Hurry! . . . Put a ring on his finger
and shoes on his feet . . .
and let us celebrate with a feast!"

LUKE 15:2–3, 11–12, 20, 22–23

Kissing his son shows that the father
welcomes him back totally.
Putting shoes on his feet
shows that he *forgives him* totally.
(Shoes were the sign of a free person;
bare feet, the sign of a slave.)
Putting a ring on his son's finger
(probably the family ring) shows that
he *restores him* to full family status.

The second half of Jesus' parable
concerns the older son.
He is "so angry" that his father

is celebrating his brother's return
that he won't even enter the house—
even though his father begs him.

Jesus ends his parable without saying
what the older son eventually does.
He ends it this way because the older son
stands for the religious leaders.
They resent the fact that Jesus
has chosen to celebrate with those
who were lost but now are found.

And so Jesus constructs his parable
in such a way that each religious leader
must write his own ending to it.
Each must decide whether or not
to go inside and join the dancing or
to stay outside and sulk.

The point of Jesus' parable is clear:
We are to forgive one another
as our heavenly Father forgives us.
We are to forgive "not seven times,
but seventy times seven" (MATTHEW 18:21–23).

"We are like beasts when we injure;
like fools when we judge;
like God when we forgive." ANONYMOUS
Which am I like most of the time?

One night Dr. Martin Luther King, Jr.,
was just dozing off when his phone rang.
The caller said, "Listen, nigger,
we've taken all we want from you.
Before next week, you'll be sorry
you ever came to Montgomery."

Suddenly, all Dr. King's fears
came crashing down upon him at once.
He didn't know what to do.
In this state of confusion and panic,
he bowed his head and prayed.
Instantly, he felt God's presence
as he had never felt it before.

Dr. King's prayer introduces us
to Jesus' *third* great teaching.
Besides teaching us *to love*
and *to forgive* as he did,
Jesus also taught us *to pray* as he did.
And how did Jesus pray?

First, he prayed *often*.
"He would go away to lonely places,
where he prayed" (LUKE 5:16).

Second, he prayed in *different settings*.
Besides praying alone,
Jesus prayed in small-group settings,
with family (Jews prayed at all meals),
and with his friends (LUKE 9:28, 22:42).
Jesus also prayed in large-group settings.

Luke says, "On the Sabbath he went
as usual to the synagogue" (LUKE 4:16).

Third, Jesus prayed in *different ways*.
Outwardly, he knelt (LUKE 22:41);
raised his eyes to heaven (JOHN 17:1);
and prayed out loud (MATTHEW 26:42).

Inwardly,
Jesus prayed in different ways also.
He prayed *free* prayers from his heart,
in his own words (JOHN 17:1).
He prayed *fixed* prayers
that had been part of the Jewish faith
for centuries.
For example, on the cross
Jesus prayed Psalm 22 (MARK 15:34).

It is significant that when the disciples
asked Jesus to show them how to pray,
he began by teaching them
a fixed prayer: the Lord's Prayer (LUKE 11:1–13).

*"The LORD said, 'I was ready
to answer my people's prayers,
but they did not pray.
I was ready for them to find me,
but they did not even try.'"* ISAIAH 65:1
*How frequently do I pray?
In what settings and in what ways?*

A famous painting portrays
George Washington kneeling in the snow,
praying for his soldiers at Valley Forge.
"They lacked everything,"
wrote General LaFayette of France.
No doubt, one of the prayers Washington
prayed was the Lord's Prayer.
Two things, especially, stand out in it.

The first is the word Jesus taught us
to use to address God: *Father (Abba)*.
Abba is the word Israeli children
still use to address their fathers.
It is an affectionate title,
much like our English word *Daddy*.
Thus Jesus taught us to address God
with the loving trust of a small child.

The second thing
that stands out in the Lord's Prayer
is its two groups of petitions:
your petitions and *our* petitions.

The first group of petitions
focuses on God and God's Kingdom:

- hallowed be *your* name,
- *your* Kingdom come,
- *your* will be done.

Some people ask, "Why do we pray
for the *coming* of God's Kingdom?

Didn't Jesus establish it?"
The answer is "Yes, but it
has not yet *come in all its fullness.*"

Here we need to recall
that the coming of the Kingdom of God
is not a one-time event but a process.
God's Kingdom is like a seed
that is planted and is growing
but has not yet borne its intended fruit.

The second group of petitions
shifts the focus of the Lord's Prayer
from *God and God's Kingdom*
to *us and our needs:*

- give *us our* daily bread,
- forgive *us our* trespasses,
- deliver *us* from evil.

These petitions ask the Father
for the basic things we need
as we work and pray daily
for the coming of the Kingdom.

Do I ever experiment
in praying the Lord's Prayer—
like praying it in a low, audible voice?
With hands extended and opened upward?
How has this affected my prayer?

211

Ancient weddings lasted for days.
A high point was the arrival
of the groom at the bride's home.
Bridesmaids carrying lighted oil lamps
went out to welcome him.

It is against this background
that Jesus tells a parable
to answer this important question:
When will God's Kingdom come and
the "Son of Man" return?

Jesus describes ten bridesmaids
waiting at the bride's home
to welcome the bridegroom.
Five of the young women are wise and
have a full supply of oil for their lamps.
Five are foolish and have a small supply.

When the bridegroom delays in coming,
the young women fall asleep
and their oil supply burns low.
The foolish ones go off to get more oil.

"The bridegroom arrived.
The five who were ready
went in with him to the wedding feast,
and the door was closed.
Later the others arrived. 'Sir, sir!
Let us in!' they cried. . . . 'I don't
know you,' the bridegroom answered."
MATTHEW 25:10–12

The point of Jesus' parable is
that it has not been given us to know
when the Kingdom will be completed
and the "Son of Man" will return.

This we do know:
Only those who are ready
will enter the wedding feast
to celebrate the coming and the fullness
of the Kingdom of God.
To those who are ready, Jesus will say:

*"Come and possess the kingdom
which has been prepared for you
ever since the creation of the world.
I was hungry and you fed me, . . .
naked and you clothed me."*
                              MATTHEW 25:35–36

To those who are not ready,
Jesus will say just the opposite.

*"Jesus hid the last day from us
so that we'd be on the lookout for him
every day of our lives."* SAINT AUGUSTINE
*If I knew that Jesus would return
in two hours,
what is one thing I would certainly do?
Why don't I do it now?*

213

Toward the end of his life,
Dr. Martin Luther King told his followers,
"We've got some difficult days ahead.
But it doesn't matter with me now. . . .
I just want to do God's will."

Toward the end of his life,
Jesus, also, warned his followers, saying:

*"The Son of Man will be handed over
to those who will kill him."* MARK 9:31

Jesus' situation is simply the climax
of an escalating conflict between him
and the religious leaders of his time.
It began when Jesus' ministry began.

One day, after healing a man, Jesus says,
"Your sins are forgiven you."
When the leaders hear this, they erupt.

*"Who is this man
who speaks such blasphemy!
God is the only one
who can forgive sins!"* LUKE 5:21

Later, when Jesus heals the hand
of a paralyzed man on the Sabbath,
the leaders erupt again.

*They were filled with rage
and began to discuss among themselves
what they could do to Jesus.* LUKE 6:11

Later, Jesus' disciples ignore the rule,
promulgated by the leaders,
that people must wash ritually
before sitting down to eat.
When the leaders blame Jesus for this,
he angers them still more by saying:

"How right Isaiah was
when he prophesied about you! . . .
These people . . . honor me
with their words, but their heart
is really far away from me. . . .
They teach human rules
as though they were my laws!" MARK 7:6–7

Finally, the day comes when the leaders
accuse Jesus of expelling demons
by the power of Beelzebul,
the chief of the demons (MARK 3:22).

[Jesus said,] "No, it is not Beelzebul,
but God's Spirit, who gives me the power
to drive out demons,
which proves that the Kingdom of God
has already come upon you." MATTHEW 12:28

"Observance without reason
is not worship, but idolatry." ANONYMOUS
What is the nature of my observance?

The gap between Jesus
and the religious leaders widens.
The breaking point finally comes
when Jesus raises Lazarus from the dead.
News of the miracle
spreads everywhere among the people.
The leaders now realize
an impossible situation is at hand.

LEADERS　　*What shall we do? . . .*
If we let him go on
in this way,
everyone will believe in him,
and the Roman authorities
will take action and destroy
our Temple and our nation! . . .

NARRATOR　　*From that day on*
the Jewish authorities
made plans to kill Jesus.
So Jesus did not
travel openly in Judea. . . .
The time
for the Passover Festival
was near,
and many people went up from
the country to Jerusalem. . . .

PEOPLE　　*What do you think?*
Surely [Jesus] will not come
to the festival, will he?

JOHN 11:47–48, 53–56

The answer is not long in coming.
Suddenly, word buzzes through the city
that Jesus is on his way to Jerusalem.

Jesus enters the city riding on a donkey.
The crowds stream out to greet him.
They cut branches from the trees,
carpet the road with them, and shout:

"Praise to David's son!
God bless him
who comes in the name of the Lord!
Praise be to God!" MATTHEW 21:9

When Jesus arrives at the Temple,
he is shocked at what he sees.
Its outer court looks like a carnival.
Sellers are hawking animals for sacrifice.
Jesus kicks over their tables and shouts:

"God said, 'My Temple
will be called a house of prayer.'
But you are making it a hideout
for thieves!" MATTHEW 21:13

What are my thoughts
as I imagine myself to be a seller
whose table full of coins
has just been kicked over by Jesus?

The Temple officials are incensed
when they see Jesus kicking over tables.
They demand an explanation.
Jesus gives it in the form of a parable.

A landowner rents his vineyard
to tenants for a share of the crops.
When harvest comes, the landowner
sends slaves to collect his share,
but the tenants kill them.

Again the owner sends other slaves,
but the tenants do the same thing.

*"Last of all he sent his son to them.
'Surely they will respect my son,' he said.
But when the tenants saw the son,
they said to themselves,
'This is the owner's son.
Come on, let's kill him, and we will get
his property!' So they grabbed him . . .
and killed him."* MATTHEW 21:37–39

Jesus ends his parable by asking
the Temple officials this question:

*"When the owner of the vineyard comes,
what will he do to those tenants?" . . .
[The officials answered,]
"He will certainly kill those evil men . . .
and will rent the vineyard out*

*to other tenants, who will give him
his share of the harvest."* MATTHEW 21:40–41

Jesus' parable of the tenants
has been called a "mini Bible," because
it sums up the entire Scripture story
in a remarkably simple way.
Its "cast of characters" is as follows:

- Landowner   God
- Vineyard   Israel
- First renting   Old Covenant

- First tenants   Religious leaders
- Slaves   Early prophets
- Other slaves   Later prophets

- Owner's son   Jesus
- Second renting   New Covenant
- Other tenants   Apostles

Jesus' confrontation with Temple officials
ends with this editorial comment:
"The chief priests and the Pharisees . . .
knew that [Jesus] was talking about them"
(MATTHEW 21:45).

*What are my thoughts
as I imagine myself to be
a Temple official who is still puzzled
about Jesus' identity?*

The story *Town Beyond the Wall*
deals with the power of a friendship
between Michael and Pedro.

The power flows
not from the friendship directly,
but from the *memory* of it.

Michael is able endure torture
because he is able to "remember"
his friend in such a profound way that
it makes Pedro mysteriously "present."

That story makes an important point.
For ancient Jews,
"remembering" a past religious event
involved more than "calling it to mind."
It involved making it present—by faith—
reliving it, and partaking
in its original power and blessing.

So when Jews celebrated the Passover,
they did more than "recall" the event
that freed them from Egyptian slavery.
By faith, they made it present,
relived it, and partook
of its original power and blessing.

It is with this understanding
that Jesus and his disciples gathered
to celebrate the Passover supper.

Normally, Jews ate two meals a day:
one in the later morning and
the other in the late afternoon.
They ate the Passover, however, at night,
at the appearance of the first stars.
Thus every Jew ate the meal
at the same time as one family.

Acting as the father,
Jesus begins the Passover meal
in an unusual and surprising way.
He pours water into a basin and
begins to wash the feet of each disciple.

For Jews, washing feet was humiliating.
Only slaves performed this task.
Jesus' action creates a deep impression.
When Jesus finishes, he says:

"I, your Lord and Teacher,
have just washed your feet.
You, then, should wash one another's feet.
I have set an example for you." JOHN 13:14–15

To what extent do I believe
this statement of an anonymous writer:
"The measure of greatness
is not the number of servants you have,
but the number of people you serve"?

Jesus introduces the Passover meal
by preparing the cup of red wine.
When it is ready, he says to the disciples:

"Take this and share it. . . .
I tell you that from now on
I will not drink this wine
until the Kingdom of God comes." LUKE 22:17–18

Red wine recalls the Passover lamb,
whose blood was used to mark
Hebrew houses and save the occupants
from the "angel of death"
the night they fled from Egypt (EXODUS 12:22).
It also recalls the "covenant blood"
that Moses sprinkled on them
at Mount Sinai (EXODUS 24:8).

Next, Jesus prepares the Passover food
to be eaten at the meal:

- bitter herbs,
- unleavened bread,
- sauce for the herbs and bread, and
- a roasted lamb.

Bitter herbs recall Israel's years
of bitter slavery in the land of Egypt.
Clay-colored *sauce* recalls the bricks
they made under the hot Egyptian sun.
Unleavened bread recalls the haste
with which they left Egypt—before the

next day's bread dough is able to rise.
The *lamb* recalls its *blood* that saved
them and its *body* that nourished them
for their journey out of Egypt.

When all is ready,
Jesus takes the bread into his hands,
give thanks to God, breaks it, and
gives it to the disciples, saying:

"This is my body,
which is given for you.
Do this in memory of me." LUKE 22:19

Identifying the bread as his body
recalls the day Jesus told the people:

"I am the living bread
that came down from heaven. . . .
The bread that I will give you
is my flesh." JOHN 6:51

As the disciples eat the "living bread,"
they sense that something marvelous
is taking place.
It is a moment they would never forget.

How do I understand these words:
"The bread we break: when we eat it,
we are sharing in the body of Christ"?
1 CORINTHIANS 10:16

The Passover meal ends
with Jesus preparing a final cup of wine.
Silence falls over the disciples
as they watch Jesus take the cup,
raise his eyes to heaven, and pray:

*"This cup is God's new covenant
sealed with my blood,
which is poured out for you."* LUKE 22:20

The disciples are struck by the phrases
"new covenant" and
"sealed with my blood."
They recall the old covenant,
when Moses sprinkled animal blood
upon the people, saying:

*"This is the blood that seals the covenant,
which the LORD made with you."*
EXODUS 24:8

They also recall God's promise:

*"I will make a new covenant
with the people of Israel."* JEREMIAH 31:31

As the disciples drink from the cup,
their minds are filled with questions:
Is this the moment God had promised?
Is this the new covenant?
What did Jesus mean when he said
"sealed with my blood"?

Mark ends his Last Supper narrative
with the words:

*Then they sang a hymn and
went out to the Mount of Olives.* MARK 14:26

As the disciples walk along with Jesus
under the starlit sky,
they are profoundly happy.
But it is a bittersweet happiness.
Jesus has said
too many sorrow-shadowed things
to allow for unrestrained joy.

These words, especially,
keep drumming and echoing in their ears:

"Do this in memory of me." LUKE 22:19

*"[Jesus said,]
'I am the living bread
that came down from heaven.
If you eat this bread,
you will live forever.' . . .
Many of his followers heard this and
said, 'This teaching is too hard' "* JOHN 6:51, 60
*To what extent, and in what way,
do I find this teaching of Jesus
hard to accept?*

Some years after the Last Supper,
Paul wrote to the Christians in Greece:

*I received from the Lord
the teaching that I passed on to you:
that the Lord Jesus,
on the night he was betrayed,
took a piece of bread,
gave thanks to God, broke it, and said,
"This is my body, which is for you.
Do this in memory of me."*

*In the same way, after the supper
he took the cup and said,
"This cup is God's new covenant,
sealed with my blood.
Whenever you drink it,
do so in memory of me."
This means that every time you eat
this bread and drink from this cup
you proclaim the Lord's death
until he comes.* 1 CORINTHIANS 11:23–26

Paul's words explain why we still
gather together to share the Lord's Supper.

*We eat bread, but not enough
to take our hunger away;
we drink wine, but not enough
to take our thirst away. . . .
The simple signs,*

which cannot satisfy our desires,
speak first of all of God's absence.
He has not yet returned. . . .

But even as we affirm his absence
we realize that he is already with us.
We say to each other, "Eat and drink,
this is his body and blood." . . .

Therefore, every time ministers
call their people around the table,
they call them to experience
not only the Lord's presence
but his absence as well;
they call them . . .
to sadness as well as to joy.

HENRI NOUWEN, *The Living Reminder*

In brief, we gather at the Lord's table
to eat the Lord's Supper because
God's Kingdom is not yet complete.
It is "present," but not in its fullness.
To borrow an image from Jesus himself,
we may say that the vine is growing,
but it has not yet borne its fruit.

When I gather at the Lord's table,
am I more conscious
of God's presence or God's absence?
How do I explain this?

The Mount of Olives lies
across the valley from Jerusalem.
A tiny cluster of ancient olive trees
stands on its slope.
Experts think that they mark the spot
where Jesus and his disciples went
after the Last Supper.

When the small group reaches the spot,
a deep sorrow comes over Jesus.
He goes off alone and prays:

"Father! All things are possible for you.
Take this cup of suffering away. . . .
Yet not what I want,
but what you want." MARK 14:36

Returning, Jesus finds the disciples asleep.
He wakes them up and says to them:

"Keep watch, and pray
that you do not fall into temptation. . . ."
He went away once more and prayed.
                                    MARK 14:38–39

Returning a final time from prayer,
Jesus says to them:

"The hour has come! . . . Get up. . . ."
Jesus was still speaking when Judas,
one of the twelve disciples, arrived.
With him was a crowd

armed with swords and clubs and
sent by [the Temple leaders].   MARK 14:41–43

Judas kisses Jesus, and Jesus says,
"Judas, is it with a kiss
that you betray the Son of Man?" (LUKE 22:48).
After a skirmish, the disciples flee.
The crowd seizes Jesus and leads him
away to the residence of the high priest.

Peter follows at a distance
and enters the high priest's courtyard.
Three times Peter is recognized
and charged with being a disciple.
Three times Peter denies the charge.
Then a rooster crows, and Peter recalls
what Jesus had said to him earlier:

"Before the rooster crows two times,
you will say three times
that you do not know me."
And he broke down and cried.   MARK 14:72

"The penalty of sin is to face,
not the anger of Jesus,
but the heartbreak in his eyes."
                        WILLIAM BARCLAY
What do I see as I imagine myself
looking into Jesus' eyes right now?

The next morning Jesus is led off
to be questioned by the Jewish Council.

COUNCIL   *Tell us, are you the Messiah?*

JESUS   *If I tell you,*
   you will not believe me. . . .
   From now on the Son of Man
   will be seated at the right side
   of Almighty God.

COUNCIL   *Are you, then, the Son of God?*

JESUS   *You say that I am.*

COUNCIL   *We don't need any witnesses!*
   We ourselves have heard
   what he said! LUKE 22:67, 69–71

The high priest in charge tears his robe
and shouts, "Blasphemy!"
Turning to the Council, he says:

"You have just heard his blasphemy!
What do you think?"
They answered, "He is guilty
and must die." MATTHEW 26:65–66

The soldiers lead Jesus off to Pilate.
They accuse him of telling the people
that he is a king and
that they should not pay taxes (LUKE 23:2).

Thus they shift the case against Jesus
from a religious one to a political one.
True, Jesus had discussed taxes,

but he did not oppose them (MATTHEW 22:15–22).
And he was called a king, but he refused
the title in a political way (JOHN 6:15).

Pilate sizes up the case
as a religious squabble among Jews.
When his efforts to free Jesus fail,
he tries a final desperate move.
He has the soldiers whip Jesus.

The soldiers not only whip Jesus
but also crown him with thorns
and ridicule him.

Then Pilate presents Jesus to the crowd.
He hopes the effects
of the cruel beating will satisfy them,
but they are not satisfied.

They shouted, . . . "Crucify him!" . . .
Then Pilate handed Jesus over to them
to be crucified. JOHN 19:15–16

Peter writes in his first letter:
"Christ himself carried our sins
in his body to the cross. . . .
By his wounds . . . you have been healed."
1 PETER 2:24

What have I done for Jesus?
What am I doing for Jesus?
What ought I to do for Jesus?

The soldiers lead Jesus away
to a place called *Golgotha,*
meaning "the place of the skull."

*Then they crucified him and
divided his clothes among themselves,
throwing dice to see who would get
which piece of clothing. . . .
They also crucified two bandits . . .
one on his right and the other on his left.*

MARK 15:24, 27

An old Polish Jew who survived
the Nazi massacre of a Warsaw ghetto
said of the crucifixion of Jesus:

*As I looked at the man
upon the cross . . .
I knew I must make up my mind . . .
and either take my stand beside him and
share in his undefeated faith in God . . .
or else fall finally into a bottomless pit
of bitterness, hatred, and . . . despair.*

S. PAUL SHILLING, *God in an Age of Atheism*

One thing that impressed the old Jew
was how Jesus turned to his Father
in prayer in the midst of his agony.
The prayer Jesus used is Psalm 22:

*"My God, my God,
why have you abandoned me?"* (22:1)

Incredibly, this psalm was written
some six hundred years before
the Romans devised crucifixion,
but it describes Jesus' situation perfectly.

I am no longer a human being;
I am a worm. . . .
All my bones are out of joint;
my heart is like melted wax.
My throat is as dry as dust. . . .

They tear at my hands and feet.
All my bones can be seen.
My enemies look at me and stare.
They gamble for my clothes
and divide them among themselves.
O LORD, don't stay away from me!
Come quickly to my rescue!
PSALM 22:6, 14–19

"It is not the physical death of Jesus
which is redemptive
but the love of Jesus. . . .
The crucified Jesus is a sign . . .
that love may suffer but it overcomes. . . .
The man of faith has found [in Jesus] . . .
a love mightier than death."
ANTHONY PADOVANO, *Who Is Christ?*
What are my thoughts as I reread
the excerpts from Psalm 22?

233

At noon the whole country
was covered with darkness,
which lasted for three hours.
At three o'clock Jesus cried out, . . .
"My God, my God,
why did you abandon me?" . . .
With a loud cry Jesus died.

The curtain hanging in the Temple
was torn in two, from top to bottom.
The army officer who was
standing there in front of the cross
saw how Jesus had died.
"This man was really the Son of God!"
he said. MARK 15:33–39

Two things stand out
in Mark's description of the crucifixion:

• the tearing of the Temple curtain and
• the army officer's act of faith.

Early Christians
interpreted the tearing of the curtain
to be a sign indicating the end of
the Old Testament Temple and
the Old Testament sacrifice (HEBREWS 10:9).

The New Testament temple and
the New Testament sacrifice
are being "born" on the cross.
The New Testament temple

is the body of Jesus (EPHESIANS 1:22–23).
The New Testament sacrifice is
Jesus' death on the cross (HEBREWS 9:14, 10:9).

The second thing that stands out
is the army officer's act of faith in Jesus.
He becomes the first
in an endless parade of people
who look at Jesus on the cross,
believe, and win eternal life.
Jesus foretold this earlier, saying:

"The Son of Man must be lifted up,
so that everyone who believes in him
may have eternal life." JOHN 3:14–15

"I carry a cross in my pocket . . .
It's not for . . . all the world to see.
It's simply an understanding
Between my Savior and me. . . .
It reminds me to be thankful
For my blessings day by day
And strive to serve Him better
In all that I do and say. . . .
Reminding no one but me
That Jesus Christ is Lord of my life
If only I'll let him be." AUTHOR UNKNOWN
What do I say to the crucified Jesus
about how I can serve him better
and how I can let him be "Lord of my life"?

A man sat in a canoe reading a book.
Glancing down, he saw a water beetle
crawling up the side of the canoe.
Halfway up, it fastened its talons
to the wood and died.
The man returned to reading his book.

Later he glanced down again.
The beetle had dried in the blazing sun,
and its back was cracking open.
As he watched,
something emerged from the opening.
It was a magnificent dragonfly.
The man took his finger
and nudged the dried-up shell.
It was like an empty tomb.

This beautiful example from nature
helps us better appreciate Easter.

NARRATOR   *As Sunday morning*
              was dawning, Mary Magdalene
              and the other Mary
              went to look at the tomb.
              Suddenly
              there was a violent earthquake;
              an angel of the Lord
              came down from heaven,
              rolled the stone away,
              and sat on it.
              His appearance was like

lightning, and his clothes
were white as snow.
The guards were so afraid
that they trembled
and became like dead men.
The angel spoke to the women.

ANGEL *I know you are looking for Jesus,*
who was crucified. . . .
Tell his disciples, . . . "He has been
raised from death. . . ."

NARRATOR *So they left the tomb . . .*
afraid and yet filled with joy,
and ran to tell his disciples.
Suddenly Jesus met them.

JESUS *Peace be with you. . . .*
Do not be afraid.
Go and tell my brothers
to go to Galilee,
and there they will see me.
       MATTHEW 28:1–5, 7–10

Meanwhile, the guards reported back
to the authorities, who told them to say
that someone stole the body
while they were dozing.

How do I understand these words:
"The gospels don't explain Easter;
Easter explains the gospels"?

The disciples' reaction to the report
of Jesus' resurrection is disbelief.
They call it "nonsense" (LUKE 24:11).
But then other appearances of Jesus
begin to take place.

On Easter Sunday evening, two disciples
are returning to their home in Emmaus.
Suddenly a stranger approaches
and walks along with them.
They tell him about the death of Jesus,
the women who found the tomb empty,
and the refusal of the disciples
to believe that Jesus is risen.

JESUS   *How foolish you are,*
              how slow you are
              to believe everything
              the prophets said! Was it not
              necessary for the Messiah
              to suffer these things
              and then enter his glory?

NARRATOR   *And Jesus explained to them*
              what was said about himself
              in all the Scriptures,
              beginning with the books
              of Moses and . . . the prophets.
              As they came near the
              village . . . , Jesus acted as if
              he were going farther;
              but they held him back

DISCIPLES   *Stay with us;*
the day is almost over
and it is getting dark.

NARRATOR   *So he went in to stay. . . .*
He sat down to eat with them,
took the bread,
and said the blessing;
then he broke the bread
and gave it to them.
Then their eyes were opened
and they recognized him,
but he disappeared
from their sight. . . .
They got up at once
and went back to Jerusalem.

LUKE 24:25–31, 33

How relevant is this prayer for me?
"Lord Jesus, look kindly on those of us
who find it hard to believe
that you are risen and alive among us.
Come to us, again, as you did
to the disciples returning to Emmaus.
Explain to us anew the Scriptures,
as you did to them.
Set afire the embers of faith
that still smolder in our hearts.
Sit down again with us at table,
in the breaking of the bread."

Easter Sunday night finds the disciples
gathered together in a room.
Suddenly Jesus appears in their midst.

NARRATOR   *The disciples*
            were filled with joy. . . .
JESUS   *Peace be with you.*
            As the Father sent me,
            so I send you.
            Receive the Holy Spirit.
            If you forgive people's sins,
            they are forgiven;
            if you do not forgive them,
            they are not forgiven. JOHN 20:19–23

Some ask, "Why did Jesus pick
Easter night to give his disciples
the power to forgive people's sins?"

The answer? It is the perfect Easter gift.
It is why Jesus died and rose,
that we might be "put right with God"
(ROMANS 5:9).

Jesus not only forgives his disciples
but also empowers them to communicate
his forgiveness to those yet unborn.

Sometime later, some of the disciples
are on an all-night fishing trip.
Returning empty-handed,
they see a stranger on the beach.

At first they ignore him.
Then the stranger calls to them,
"Throw your net in on the right side."
They do and it fills up with fish.
John stares at the stranger and gasps.
Jesus is cooking fish over a fire.

After the disciples pull ashore
and take care of their catch of fish,
they sit down and eat with Jesus.
Then Jesus does something beautiful.
He asks Peter three times,
"Do you love me?"
Three times Peter says, "Yes, Lord!"
Three times Jesus says, "Feed my sheep!"

Peter's three affirmations of love
erase his three denials of Jesus.
Jesus' three responses "Feed my sheep!"
commission Peter to be the shepherd
of the flock of Jesus' followers (JOHN 21).

*"Jesus impacted the lives
of his followers more powerfully
after his death than before it."* ANONYMOUS
*What are my thoughts
as I imagine myself to be Peter,
lying in bed that night,
reflecting on what happened
on the beach that morning?*

7 World of Pentecost _____

MEDITERRANEAN
SEA

• Sidon

• Tyre   • Caesarea Philippi

• Capernaum
Cana • • Tiberias   SEA OF
• Nazareth   GALILEE
▲
Mount Tabor

• Caesarea

SAMARIA   • Gerasa

                          Jordan River

• Joppa

Emmaus •
Jerusalem •
        • Qumram
      • Bethlehem

JUDEA   DEAD
                              SEA

                              NABATEA

During the Cold War,
East Berlin communist officials
built a giant television tower
with a revolving restaurant on top of it.
It was supposed to be a showpiece
to the West, but a design fluke turned it
into an embarrassment to the East.

When the sun hit it at a certain angle,
it became a dazzling cross.
Officials tried repainting the tower
to "blot out" the cross, but to no avail.

Something similar happens
after Jesus' crucifixion on Calvary.
Jesus' opponents hope his death
will "blot out" Christianity,
but just the opposite happens.

Christianity spreads so swiftly
that by 64 C.E. it is flourishing
as far away as Rome itself.
The story of its amazing spread is told
in the Acts of the Apostles. Luke begins:

In my first book
I wrote about all the things
that Jesus did and taught from the time
he began his work until the day
he was taken up to heaven. . . .
For forty days after his death

he appeared . . . many times in ways
that proved beyond doubt
that he was alive. . . .
[Jesus' final words to his disciples are:]
"When the Holy Spirit comes upon you,
you will be filled with power,
and you will be witnesses for me
in Jerusalem,
in all of Judea and Samaria, and
to the ends of the earth." ACTS 1:1–3, 8

Jesus' final words, concerning where
his disciples should witness to him,
give Luke the outline for Acts:

- Jerusalem witness   chapters 1–7
- Judea-Samaria witness   chapters 8–12
- world witness   chapters 13–28

After Jesus disappears from sight,
two heavenly figures appear, saying:

"This Jesus . . . will come back
in the same way
that you saw him go to heaven." ACTS 1:11

"Someday I will be judged
not on my earthly achievements,
but on my witness to Jesus." ANONYMOUS
How do I evaluate my witness so far?

245

*The apostles went back to Jerusalem
from the Mount of Olives,
which is about half a mile away. . . .
[In the days ahead they met] frequently
to pray as a group,
together with the women
and with Mary the mother of Jesus
and with his brothers.* ACTS 1:12, 14

One day
while they are waiting and praying for
the coming of the Holy Spirit,
Peter suggests
they choose a replacement for Judas
to bring the number of apostles
back up to twelve.
They agree that the replacement
must have the following qualifications:

*"He must be one of the men
who were in our group during
the whole time that the Lord Jesus
traveled about with us,
beginning from the time John preached
his message of baptism until the day
Jesus was taken . . . to heaven."*

*So they proposed two men:
Joseph, who was called Barsabbas
(also known as Justus), and Matthias.
Then they prayed, "Lord, . . . show us*

which of these two you have chosen
to serve as an apostle. . . ."
They drew lots . . . and the one chosen
was Matthias. ACTS 1:21–26

Drawing lots was not unusual for Jews
(JOSHUA 18:6, JUDGES 20:9).
They used it to keep personal feelings
from influencing social decisions.
But beyond this,
it puts an outcome in the hands of God.
If God has a preference about something,
drawing lots is a way to let God show it.
For biblical Jews, God's will
is more important than life itself.

How important to me
is discerning and doing God's will?
For example, how fervently
can I pray the following prayer?
"Lord, teach me to be generous.
Teach me to serve you as you deserve;
to give and not to count the cost;
to fight and not to heed the wounds;
to toil and not to seek for rest;
to labor and not to ask for reward,
except to know
that I am doing your will."
                Attributed to SAINT IGNATIUS OF LOYOLA

247

A little boy received a toy sailboat
for his birthday. He was so excited
that he ran to the window,
looked up to the sky, and shouted,
"O God! Have you seen my boat?"

A pause followed,
as if he were waiting for God's answer.
Then, turning to his mother, he asked,
"What is God like?"
Before she could respond, he blurted out,
"I know! God is like the wind!"

Ancient Jews would have applauded
the little boy's insight,
for they also saw a parallel
between the *wind* and God.
The wind's featherlike touch and
its tornadolike force spoke to them
of God's gentleness (1 KINGS 19:12) and
God's power (JOB 38:1).

Ancient Jews also saw a parallel
between *fire* and God.

This parallel grew out of
Moses' experience of God speaking
from the burning bush and
Israel's experience of God descending
amid fire on Mount Sinai (EXODUS 19:16–18).
It is against this biblical background

that we should read Luke's description
of the Pentecost event.

Suddenly there was a noise . . .
like a strong wind blowing. . . .
Then they saw what looked like
tongues of fire which spread out
and touched each person there.
They were all filled with the Holy Spirit
and began to talk in other languages, as
the Spirit enabled them to speak. ACTS 2:2–4

The "noise from the sky"
attracts a crowd of people to the place
where the disciples are gathered.
When they hear the disciples speaking,
they can't believe their ears, saying:

"Some of us are from Crete and Arabia—
yet all of us hear them
speaking in our own languages. . . .
What does this mean?" ACTS 2:11–12

What *are my thoughts*
as I imagine myself to be in the crowd
listening to the disciples
speaking a different language than mine,
but in a way that I can understand?
How do I answer the question
"What does this mean?" Why?

249

William Bradford was a Pilgrim
who came over on the *Mayflower* in 1620.
As governor of the Plymouth Colony,
he proclaimed the first Thanksgiving Day
celebrated in America.

Ancient Jews
also celebrated a "Thanksgiving Day."
Called *Pentecost* (meaning "fiftieth"),
it came fifty days after Passover
and was a time for thanking God

- for the yearly harvest and
- for the Sinai covenant.

The celebration
took place in the Jerusalem Temple.
People who lived near Jerusalem went
to the Temple to celebrate the feast.
People who lived far from Jerusalem
tried to celebrate the feast
in the Temple
at least once during their lifetime.

This explains why people
speaking many different languages
were in Jerusalem on Pentecost.

It also brings up the question that
everyone was asking when they heard
the apostles speaking
in their own particular foreign language:

"What does this mean?" (ACTS 2:12).
The clue to the answer
is found in the Book of Genesis.

Recall that before the sin (pride)
that produced the Tower of Babel event,
people are portrayed
as speaking the same language (GENESIS 11:1).

After the sin, God is portrayed
as mixing up their language and
scattering them over the earth (GENESIS 11:9).

The Pentecost event is depicted
as reversing the Babel event.
What sin tragically disunites then,
the Holy Spirit gloriously reunites now.

And so what happened on Pentecost
is an event of historic importance
for all peoples—not just Jews.

The coming of the Holy Spirit
marks a milestone
in God's dealings not only with Israel,
but with all people.
The *de-creation* of the world by sin
is being replaced by the *re-creation*
of the world by the Holy Spirit.

Why is the human race still so disunited?

The Holy Spirit's coming
sheds light on many things,
just as Jesus foretold it would:

*"The Holy Spirit . . . . will teach you
everything and make you remember
all that I have told you."* JOHN 14:26

It is against this background
that we listen to Peter's explanation
of the Pentecost event to the crowd:

*"Fellow Jews . . . , listen to me and
let me tell you what this means. . . .
This is what
the prophet Joel spoke about:
'This is what I will do
in the last days, God says:
I will pour out my Spirit on everyone . . .
and they will proclaim my message . . .
before the great and glorious
Day of the Lord comes.
And then, whoever calls out to the Lord
for help will be saved.'"* ACTS 2:14, 16–18, 20–21

The title "Day of the Lord"
refers to that moment in history
when Jews believe
God will intervene in their behalf.
It is the day when God's power and glory
will manifest itself to all the world.

Much as Christians think of history
as being divided
into *before* and *after Christ,*
ancient Jews thought of it as divided
into *before* and *after* the *Day of the Lord.*

Peter sees Pentecost
as the *beginning* of the *Day of the Lord,*
which will *end* with the day of Jesus'
final coming at the end of history.

Peter's words move the people deeply.
They ask, "What shall we do?" Peter says:

*"You must turn away
from your sins and be baptized
in the name of Jesus Christ,
so that your sins will be forgiven;
and you will receive . . . the Holy Spirit."
About three thousand people were added
to the group that day.* ACTS 2:38, 41

*"Salvation is not something
that is done for you but something
that happens within you.
It is not the clearing of a court record
but the transformation of a life attitude."*
ALBERT W. PALMER
*Had I been present when Peter spoke,
what might I have done?*

Week 17: **The Spirit Comes**

Day 6: **Sermons in Acts**

No tape recorder was running
during Peter's sermon on Pentecost.
No scribe was assigned to take notes.
This raises an important question.

How did Luke go about composing
Peter's sermon—and others—in Acts?
(About a third of the book is sermons
and direct address.)

Luke probably did
what the historians of his time did.
He reconstructed the sermons
and the direct address.

For example, the historian Thucydides,
who lived centuries before Luke, says:

*I found it hard
to recall the precise words
I heard spoken at an event.
The same is true of those
who gave me reports of an event.
So I put in the mouths of the speakers
what I thought to be most opportune
for them to say in the given situation.
At the same time,
I have kept as closely as possible
to the general sense
of what was actually said by them.*

History of the Peloponnesian War

The sermons and speeches in Acts
are probably shorter than the originals,
perhaps only a summary of them.

In some cases—
as in the "we" sections (16:10–17, 20:5–21),
where Luke was traveling with Paul—
Luke may have kept excellent notes,
scribbled in a "travel journal."

In other cases, Luke had to rely
on the recollections of others.
Here we need to recall Luke's purpose.

Luke does not so much write
a "history" of the early Church,
or an early Christian apologetic,
as he does a theological essay
that describes, somewhat idyllically,
the character, growth, and
problems of the early Church.
       RICHARD DILLON and JOSEPH FITZMYER,
           "Acts of the Apostles"

Can I recall some event in my life
where I cannot recall
the exact words that were spoken,
but where I can recall
the idea or spirit of what was said?
What point does that fact make?

A mother took her five-year-old son
to a concert by Ignace Paderewski,
hoping it would encourage her son
in his own musical efforts.
She was delighted to see
how close to the stage their seats were.

Then she met an old friend
and got so involved talking with her
that she failed to notice her son
wandering away to do some exploring.

When eight o'clock arrived,
the lights dimmed slowly,
the audience hushed,
and the spotlight came on.
Only then did the woman see her son
sitting at the piano on the stage,
picking out
"Twinkle, Twinkle, Little Star."

She gasped in total disbelief.
But before she could retrieve the boy,
Paderewski walked onto the stage.

Tiptoeing over to the piano,
Paderewski whispered to the boy,
"Don't stop! Keep playing!"
Then the great pianist
took his own left hand
and began filling in the bass.

A few seconds later, he reached around
the other side of the boy
and added a running obbligato
(minor melody enhancing the major one).

Together, the maestro and the boy
entertained the audience.
When they finished,
a thunderous applause broke out.

Years later, people couldn't remember
every piece Paderewski played that night,
but they all remembered
"Twinkle, Twinkle, Little Star."

The image of the mature maestro
and the immature boy at the piano
is a magnificent image
of the Holy Spirit and the Church,
uniting to make beautiful music.

*"Alone we are only a spark,
but in the Spirit we are a fire.
Alone we are only a string,
but in the Spirit we are a lyre. . . .
Alone we are only a feather,
but in the Spirit we are a wing."*
  Inspired by Mexican mystic AMADO NERVO
*What special message might the story
of Padarewski and the boy hold for me?*

Peter Matthiessen and a friend
were hiking in a third-world country.
Suddenly they came upon a crippled girl
dragging herself along a gravel road.
Her mouth literally touched the stones.

Peter's friend told him that beggars
were known to break their children's
knees to achieve this pathetic effect
for business purposes.

Poverty and begging have always been
a tragic part of the human scene.
One day Peter and John were entering
the Temple, and a crippled beggar
asked them for money.

PETER   *I have no money at all,*
          but I give you what I have:
          in the name of Jesus Christ . . .
          get up! . . .
NARRATOR *At once the man's feet and*
          ankles became strong;
          he jumped up . . . and started
          walking around. . . .
          The people . . .
          were all surprised and amazed.
                                    ACTS 3:6–10

The news spreads throughout Jerusalem
that the healing power of Jesus

is now operating through his followers.
The news sets off a firestorm.

*Sick people
were carried out into the streets . . .
and they were all healed.* ACTS 5:15–16

The reaction of Jewish authorities
is predictable.
They arrest the apostles and
order them not to preach and heal.

PETER *We must obey God, not men. . . .*
NARRATOR *When the members
of the Council heard this,
they were . . . furious.*
GAMALIEL *Fellow Israelites, be careful
what you do to these men. . . .
Leave them alone!
If what they have planned
and done is of human origin,
it will disappear,
but if it comes from God,
you cannot possibly defeat them. . . .*
NARRATOR *The Council
followed Gamaliel's advice.*
ACTS 5:29, 33, 35, 38–39

*Do I think history has concluded that
Christianity comes from God, not humans?*

The young Church grew rapidly,
creating a need for organization.
Seven "deacons" were chosen to manage
the Church's *material* needs.
This freed the apostles to give full time
to its *spiritual* needs (ACTS 6:1–7).

One of the "deacons" chosen was Stephen.
"Richly blessed by God and full of power,"
he worked "great miracles and wonders
among the people" (ACTS 6:8).

[One day] members
of the synagogue of the Freedmen . . .
started arguing with Stephen. . . .
When he spoke, they could not refute him.
So they bribed some men to say,
"We heard him speaking
against Moses and against God!". . .
The High Priest asked Stephen,
"Is this true?" ACTS 6: 9, 10–11; 7:1

Stephen begins his defense by tracing
the history of God's dealings with Israel.
He shows how their ancestors
"resisted the Holy Spirit" (ACTS 7:51).

For example, God's servant Joseph
was sold into slavery by his brothers.
God's servant Moses was opposed
by the Israelites in the desert.

God's servants the prophets
were persecuted and killed by the people.
Then Stephen concludes by saying,
"And now you have betrayed and
murdered [God's Son]" (ACTS 7:52).

The members of the synagogue explode.
They drag Stephen out of the city and
stone him. Stephen's dying words are,
"Do not remember
this sin against them!" (ACTS 7:60).
And so, even in death, Stephen tries
to imitate his Master, who also forgave
his executioners (LUKE 23:34).

The death of Stephen, the first martyr
of the Church, sparks more persecutions.

[As a result,] all the believers,
except the apostles,
were scattered throughout the provinces
of Judea and Samaria. . . .
The believers who were scattered
went everywhere,
preaching the message.   ACTS 8:1, 4

How are these words of the second-century
Christian Tertullian realized
in Stephen: "The blood of martyrs
is the seed of the Church"?

Dr. Charles Townes won a Nobel prize
for his work with the laser beam.
A breakthrough in his work
came accidentally, while he was sitting
on a park bench studying some flowers.

History shows that many other
discoveries and advances in history
owe their origin to apparent accidents
rather than to human design.

An example of this is the first major
missionary outreach of Christianity.
Had Christians not been persecuted in
Jerusalem, they would not have gone out—
at least as early as they did—
to preach the message of Jesus
in Samaria and Judea.

One of the seven "deacons," chosen by
the members of the early Church,
spearheaded the outreach.

Philip went to the principal city
in Samaria and preached. . . .
Evil spirits came out from many people . . .
and many paralyzed and lame people
were healed. . . .
So there was great joy in that city. . . .
The apostles in Jerusalem
heard that the people of Samaria

had received the word of God,
so they sent Peter and John to them.

When they arrived,
they prayed for the believers
that they might receive the Holy Spirit.
For the Holy Spirit
had not yet come down on any of them;
they had only been baptized
in the name of the Lord Jesus.

Then Peter and John
placed their hands on them,
and they received the Holy Spirit.

ACTS 8:5, 7–8, 14–17

And so Peter and John
"confirm" the Samaritan Christians,
sharing with them the gift of the Spirit
they themselves received on Pentecost.

Peter and John went back to Jerusalem.
On their way
they preached the Good News
in many villages in Samaria. ACTS 8:25

Do I sense any significance
in the fact that many great advances
in history and in the Church
owe their origin to apparent accidents
rather than to human design?

Pagan gods and religious superstition
were widespread in Philip's day.
Spiritually sensitive Gentiles
grew increasingly dissatisfied
with the "religious" scene of the time.

As a result, many looked to Judaism,
with its one God and lofty moral code.
And so "searching" Gentiles
began to frequent Jewish synagogues
to pray and ponder the Scriptures.

Some of these "searchers" converted
and were called *proselytes* (ACTS 13:43).
Others simply attended the synagogue
and were called *God-fearers* (ACTS 10:2).

One God-fearer was an Ethiopian official.
Philip chanced upon him, one day,
just as the official was preparing to
return to Egypt after visiting Jerusalem.
The official was in his carriage
reading this prophetic passage
from the Book of Isaiah:

*"He was like a sheep
that is taken to be slaughtered,
like a lamb that makes no sound
when its wool is cut off. . . .
He was humiliated,
and justice was denied him. . . ."*

The official asked Philip, "Tell me,
of whom is the prophet saying this?
Of himself or of someone else?"

Then Philip began to speak;
starting from this passage of scripture,
he told him the Good News about Jesus.

As they traveled down the road,
they came to a place
where there was some water,
and the official said,
"Here is some water.
What is to keep me from being baptized?"

The official
ordered the carriage to stop,
and both Philip and the official
went down into the water,
and Philip baptized him. ACTS 8:32–38

"Amazing grace! how sweet the sound
That saved a wretch like me. . . .
How precious did the grace appear
The hour I first believed. . . .
'Tis grace that brought me safe thus far,
And grace will lead me home." JOHN NEWTON
Can I recall "the hour I first believed,"
when I first sensed grace acting
in my life in a more-than-ordinary way?

At a critical point in the Civil War,
the morale of the Northern troops
was dangerously low.
President Lincoln studied his generals
and concluded there was only one man
who could rally and revitalize them.
That general was McClellan.

McClellan saddled his great black horse
and rode off to Virginia.

*He cantered down the dusty roads and
met the heads of the retreating columns,
and he cried words of encouragement
and swung his little cap,
and he gave the beaten men
what no other man alive
could have given them—
enthusiasm, hope, confidence. . . .*

*Down mile after mile of Virginia roads
the stumbling columns came alive, and
threw caps and knapsacks into the air,
and yelled . . .
because they saw this dapper little rider
outlined against the purple starlight.*

*And this, in a way,
was the turning point of the war. . . .
And American history
would be different forever after.*
BRUCE CATTON, *This Hallowed Ground*

A similar turning point took place
in the early days of Christianity.

At that time,
the city of Caesarea-on-the-Sea
was the headquarters of the Roman army.
An officer stationed there
was a "God-fearer" named Cornelius (ACTS 10:2).

One day, while praying,
Cornelius has a spiritual experience.
An "angel" appears and instructs him
to send for Peter, who is preaching
to the south in Joppa.
Cornelius is overjoyed.
Making inquiries, he locates Peter
and sends for him.

Cornelius can hardly wait.
He senses something important
is about to take place.
Cornelius is right.
His meeting with Peter will be
a turning point
not only in his own life
but also in the life of the young Church.

What was a major turning point
in my own personal life? How did it
happen? What is one way it affected me?

Three delegates from Cornelius
reach Peter's house about noon.
They explain their mission, saying:

"Cornelius sent us. . . .
He is a good man who worships God
and is highly respected
by all the Jewish people.
An angel of God told him
to invite you to his house,
so that he could hear
what you have to say." ACTS 10:22

And so Peter and the delegation
set out for Cornelius's house.
What happens when they reach it
becomes a turning point in Christianity.

Peter begins to preach,
and suddenly the Holy Spirit
descends upon all the Gentiles present.
They begin to speak in strange tongues
and praise God.
Peter says to the Jews present:

"These people have received
the Holy Spirit, just as we also did.
Can anyone, then, stop them
from being baptized with water?"

So he ordered them to be baptized
in the name of Jesus Christ. ACTS 10:47–48

And so the Holy Spirit
descends upon the early believers
by three distinct stages:

- on *Jews* in Jerusalem (ACTS 2:4),
- on *half-Jews* in Samaria (ACTS 8:17),
- on *Gentiles* in Caesarea (ACTS 10:44).

Significantly, it is Peter who presides
over each "Pentecost."

A dispute develops, however, when
a conservative wing of Jewish Christians
says that Gentiles should be circumcised
before they are baptized.
To resolve the matter, the apostles call
the first Church council in history.

After prayerful deliberation, they decide
against requiring circumcision, saying,
"The Holy Spirit and we have agreed not
to put any other burden on you" (ACTS 15:28).

This sentence is a beautiful expression
of the Church's faith that the Holy Spirit
is in its midst, guiding it
when it gathers, especially, in council.

*How firmly do I believe the Spirit
continues to guide the Church,
especially in our time?*

269

An old Roman coin shows an ox facing
an altar and a plow. The inscription
on the coin reads, "Ready for either."
In other words, the ox must be ready
for swift sacrifice on an altar
or for the hard life of pulling a plow.

The ox's fate dramatizes the situation
that faced early Christians:
a swift death by the persecutor's sword
or a long life of struggle and hostility.

One Christian who died swiftly
was James. Acts says:

King Herod . . . had James, the brother
of John, put to death by the sword.
When he saw that this pleased the Jews,
he went ahead and had Peter arrested.

ACTS 12:1–3

Peter's imprisonment was short lived.
One night a strange light lit his cell.

An angel of the Lord stood there. . . .
At once the chains
fell off Peter's hands. . . .
He went to the home of Mary,
the mother of John Mark, where many
people had gathered and were praying. . . .
He explained to them how
the Lord had brought him out of prison.

"Tell this to James
and the rest of the believers," he said;
then he left and went somewhere else.
ACTS 12:7, 12, 17

Two points stand out in this account.

First, the statement
"he left and went somewhere else"
marks Peter's departure in Acts.

Except for a brief mention in connection
with the first Church council,
Peter disappears from public sight.
Presumably, a price was on his head,
and he judged his public presence
in Jerusalem too great a danger
to the rest of the Christian community.
A fourth-century historian, Eusebius,
says Peter eventually went to Rome,
where he was martyred years later.

The second point that stands out is
Peter's instruction to tell "James"
(not John's brother).
It introduces us to the person
who will assume leadership of
the Jerusalem church after Peter leaves.

What are my thoughts as I imagine
myself to be Peter leaving Jerusalem?

8 World of Paul

Weeks

Timeline (key dates, traditional—C.E.)

Bible (key book)
Acts (9:1–28:31)

MACEDONIA

ASIA MINOR

Thessalonica

Philippi

Berea

Troas

GALATIA

Ephesus

• Iconium
• Lystra
Tarsus
• Derbe

Athens

• Colossae

Corinth

Antioch•

CYPRUS

SYRIA

CRETE

Damascus•

MEDITERRANEAN
SEA

JUDEA

Jerusalem •

EGYPT

Every great movement in history
has its champion, someone who appears
at just the right time to spearhead it.

Organized labor had Samuel Gompers.
Women's suffrage had Susan B. Anthony.
Civil rights had Dr. Martin Luther King, Jr.
Ecumenism had Pope John XXIII.
Christianity had Paul of Tarsus.

Ironically, Paul began his life
as a mortal enemy of Christianity.

*Saul [Paul's Jewish name]
tried to destroy the church;
going from house to house,
he dragged out the believers,
both men and women,
and threw them into jail.* ACTS 8:3

One day Paul was going to Damascus
on his mission of persecution.
Suddenly a light flashed from the sky.
He fell to the ground, and a voice said:

*"Saul, Saul! Why do you persecute me?"
"Who are you, Lord?" he asked.
"I am Jesus, whom you persecute,"
the voice said. . . .
"Go into the city, where you will be told
what you must do."* ACTS 9:4–6

Temporarily blinded by the light,
Paul is led by his friends into the city.
There a Christian named Ananias
lays hands on him and his sight returns.
Paul believes in Jesus and is baptized.

Afire with his new faith,
Paul begins to preach that Jesus
is "the Son of God" (ACTS 9:20).

Paul's witness to Jesus is so powerful
that opponents of Christianity
plot to kill him.

Paul's friends get wind of the plot
and smuggle him back to Jerusalem.
But then his troubles really begin.

Jerusalem Christians doubt his sincerity.
His opponents, on the other hand,
are embarrassed by his witness.

Paul's situation grows so dangerous
that he is forced to flee to Caesarea and,
eventually, to Tarsus, his birthplace.
There he stays for a prolonged period,
pondering and praying.

*What would Paul have pondered and
prayed over, especially, during his
enforced exile in Tarsus?*

The persecution of Jerusalem Christians
scattered them to cities
as far away as Antioch in Syria.

Antioch was on the Orontes River,
near the Mediterranean Sea.
Breezes blew in from the Mediterranean
to give the city a delightful climate.

Moreover, its nearness to the sea
made it popular with tourists and sailors.
One ancient writer says
you could sit in downtown Antioch
and literally watch the world go by.

Antioch's popularity, however,
brought the city a lot of problems.
At one point in history,
the city became so wild and immoral
that one Roman general
ruled it "off limits" to his troops.

It is to this "immoral" city
that Christians brought the Good News
of Jesus, the Son of God. Acts says:

The Lord's power was with them,
and a great number of people
believed and turned to the Lord.
The news about this
reached the church in Jerusalem,
so they sent Barnabas to Antioch.

*When he . . . saw how God had blessed
the people, he was glad.* ACTS 11:21–23

Barnabas remembers Paul,
who is living a life of prayerful reflection
in Tarsus in Cilicia.
He decides to get Paul to help him.

*When he found him,
he took him to Antioch,
and for a whole year the two
met with the people of the church
and taught a large group.
It was at Antioch that the believers
were first called Christians.* ACTS 11:26

And so the early Church imitates Jesus,
who said, "People who are well
do not need a doctor" (MARK 2:17).
Like Jesus, the early Church reaches out,
especially, to society's "morally sick."
And many respond by opening their hearts
to grace and being converted.

*"To preach to people who are not ready
is a waste of time. But not to preach
to people who are ready
is a waste of human beings."* CONFUCIUS
*What is one way an ordinary person
might help to "reach out" and "preach"
to society's "morally sick"?*

In the church of Antioch . . .
were some prophets and teachers. . . .
The Holy Spirit said to them,
"Set apart for me Barnabas and Saul [Paul],
to do the work to which I have
called them." They fasted and prayed,
placed their hands on them,
and sent them off. ACTS 13:1–3

The two begin by going to Cyprus,
where Barnabas was born.
There they preach in synagogues and
even before the governor of the island.

Next they go to Asia Minor (Turkey)
and preach in such cities
as Perga, Iconium, and Lystra.
At Lystra, Paul heals a crippled man.
When the crowds see this, they exclaim:

"The gods have become like men
and have come down to us!"
They gave Barnabas the name Zeus,
and Paul the name Hermes,
because he was the chief speaker. ACTS 14:11–12

Why this surprising reaction?
A clue might be the writings of Ovid.
This poet describes a legendary visit
of Zeus and Hermes to Lystra.
The two gods come in disguise

and are badly treated by everyone
except one elderly couple.
Before leaving Lystra, the gods
punish the hostile townspeople
and reward the elderly couple.
Perhaps the citizens of Lystra
remembered this legend and did not
want to make the same mistake again.

The preaching of Paul and Barnabas
is cut short
by the arrival of influential Jews
who oppose their Christian message.
Violence erupts and Paul is stoned.
After Paul recovers,
he and Barnabas go to Derbe.
There they continue their preaching.

Eventually the time comes
for Paul and Barnabas to return home.
They have been on the road for four years
and are badly in need of a rest.
The date is 49 C.E.

*"Faith is a gift of God which we can
neither give nor take away by promises
of rewards or menaces of torture."*
THOMAS HOBBES
*How am I using my gift of faith
at this critical moment in history?*

Never have so many military veterans
returned to so many battlefields
as have the servicemen of World War II.
They return to Europe,
to the Philippines,
and to the islands of the South Pacific.

One serviceman has returned to the
Philippines four times. He explains why:
"Because this is where the most exciting
events of my life took place."

Months after Paul returns home,
he feels the urge to return to the cities
where he has preached earlier.
He takes with him a Jerusalem Christian
named Silas (1 THESSALONIANS 1:1).
Thus begins his "second missionary trip."

Upon his return to Lystra,
Paul meets a young man named Timothy.
Timothy joins Paul and Silas and
becomes a coworker and a recipient
of two of Paul's famous letters.

The three preach in town after town,
ending up in Troas.
There Paul has a vision calling
the missionaries to Macedonia (ACTS 16:9).
So they revise their plans and head
for Macedonia (European mainland).

They go to the city of Philippi,
where they make a number of converts.
There they are jailed briefly
for expelling a demon from a slave girl.
(Her powerful owners
were exploiting her for money reasons.)

Next, Paul and Silas go to Thessalonica.

There during three Sabbaths
[Paul] held discussions with the people,
quoting and explaining the Scriptures,
and proving from them that the Messiah
had to suffer and rise from death.
"This Jesus whom I announce to you,"
Paul said, "is the Messiah." ACTS 17:2–3

Paul's words convince many,
but others oppose him violently.
The situation grows so ugly
that Paul's converts fear for his life.
And so, under cover of darkness,
they hustle Silas and Paul off to Berea.
Paul and Silas preach briefly in Berea.
Then Paul sets out ahead to Athens.

Where did some of the most exciting
events of my life take place?
Which of these events would I like
to revisit and why?

"An old lady in slippers,
sitting by the fireside"—that's how
a writer described Athens in Paul's time.
But there was still beauty in the old city.

One sight that surely touched
Paul's poetic soul was the Acropolis.
This amazing mountain of rock still juts
to the height of a fifty-story building.

Paul would have shielded his eyes
from the bright Greek sun to admire
two structures on it, especially.

The first was the Parthenon,
whose ruins still stand today.
The second was a statue of Athena.
It towered so high above the horizon
that sailors far out at sea
could spot the reflection of the sun
off the spear and helmet of Athena.

But Paul did more than go sightseeing
as he waited for Silas and Timothy.
He preached in synagogues,
taught in the public square, and debated
Epicureans and Stoics (ACTS 17:16–18).

Epicureans followed Epicurus (300 B.C.E.),
who held life to be the result
of a chance coming together of atoms.
He believed the goal of life was pleasure.

But he didn't mean just *sense pleasure*.
Spiritual pleasure (virtue)
was more desirable in the long run,
because it gave greater contentment.
He held death to be the breakup of atoms
and the idea of an afterlife to be absurd.

Stoics, on the other hand, followed Zeno.
He held that life came from a "fiery" Spirit.
Human beings were like "sparks"
thrown from it. After glowing for a while,
they fell back into the Spirit,
much as sparks fall back into a bonfire.

Stoics held that the Spirit had no feelings.
Otherwise people could make it sad or
glad and, to that degree, control it.
Stoics believed we should imitate
the Spirit and banish all feeling from life,
accepting whatever happens:
"If you can't get what you want,
then learn to want what you can get."

The Athenians responded to the Gospel
as people still do: some believed,
some did not, most ignored it (ACTS 17:32–34).

If I had five minutes on prime-time TV
to explain why I follow Jesus,
what would I say?

Corinth was a wild port city.
Gamblers, prostitutes, and criminals
operated boldly on its street corners.

*To a city like this Paul dared to go
and preach "Blessed are the poor . . . !
Blessed are the clean of heart . . . !"
What could this small and helpless David
expect to achieve
against the armor-clad Goliath? . . .*

*Paul was determined to try. He knew
he would find corruption in Corinth but
not the arrogance and pride of Athens,
and he feared pride of the intellect
much more than pride of the flesh.*
GIUSEPPE RICCIOTTI, *Paul the Apostle*

Paul begins preaching in the synagogue
to Jews like himself.
Then a major blessing occurs. Acts says:

*The leader of the synagogue . . .
believed in the Lord,
together with all his family. . . .
[Following his conversion]
many other people in Corinth
heard the message,
believed, and were baptized.* ACTS 18:8

Jewish opponents of Paul are furious
and try to stop him from preaching.

They seize him and bring him
before Gallio, the Roman governor.

*"This man," they said, "is trying to
persuade people to worship God in a way
that is against the law!"* ACTS 18:13

Gallio dismisses the case, saying,
"You yourselves must settle it. I will not
be the judge of such things!" (ACTS 18:15).

Paul stays in Corinth a year and a half.
As a result, a considerable community
of Christians develops and grows.

The day finally comes, however,
when Paul decides to return to Antioch.
He bids his beloved Corinthians farewell
and promises
to keep in touch with them by letter.
The time is autumn 52 C.E.

*How might the following saying
of Bernard Baruch
be applied to Paul in a special way?
"[We] would be vastly poorer
if it had not been for men and women
who were willing to take risks
against the longest odds."
What might I risk for the Gospel today?*

A missionary on a Pacific island
says the easiest person on the island
to convert is the tribal witch doctor.
This is because
the witch doctor already believes deeply
in a spiritual world.

The missionary's experience
helps us understand how Paul
could preach in a town for six weeks
and leave behind a believing community.

All Paul had to do, in many cases,
was to refocus their spiritual vision.
They already
believed deeply in a spiritual world.

This is certainly true of the Ephesians,
whom Paul visits around 55 C.E.
They are already deeply spiritual,
worshiping the goddess Artemis.

Paul preaches in Ephesus two years.
During this period
he also visits Colossae, to whose Christians
he later sends a letter.

Paul's stay in Ephesus ends abruptly
after a near riot between Christians
and worshipers of Artemis.
From Ephesus, Paul goes to Troas,
where Luke joins him.

A high point of Paul's Troas visit
comes one Saturday night
when the believers are gathered
for the fellowship meal.

A young man named Eutychus
falls from the third-story window and
is saved from death by Paul (ACTS 20:7–12).

Luke's record
of that night preserves for us
not only a dramatic story about Paul
but also a description of how
early Christians celebrated the Eucharist.

They did so on the Lord's Day
during a "fellowship meal" together.
Paul also refers to this procedure
in 1 Corinthians 11:20–25.

Eventually Paul and Luke leave Troas and
begin the long return trip to Jerusalem.
The year is 58 C.E.

*"Christianity
is the spirit of Jesus Christ
at work in the world."* ANONYMOUS
*What are some concrete signs
that the spirit of Jesus Christ
is at work in my life, right now?*

Several political prisoners
stood before a Russian firing squad.
Just before the order "Fire!" was given,
a messenger rode up.
He carried a letter commuting
their sentences from death to hard labor.
One prisoner was Feodor Dostoevski.
He went on to write
some of the world's greatest literature.

Paul had a similar narrow escape.
It occurred after his return to Jerusalem.
A group of his opponents accused him
of speaking against the Law of Moses
and defiling the Temple.

They said this because they had seen
Trophimus from Ephesus with Paul . . .
and they thought that Paul
had taken him into the Temple. . . .

The people . . . grabbed Paul,
and dragged him out of the Temple. . . .
The mob was trying to kill Paul,
when a report was sent up to
the commander of the Roman troops. . . .
The commander took some officers and
soldiers and rushed down. ACTS 21:29–32

To avert a full-blown riot,
the commander takes Paul into custody.

The next day Paul is taken
before the Jewish Council and questioned.

The argument became so violent that
the commander . . . ordered his soldiers
to . . . get Paul away from them. ACTS 23:10

When night falls, Paul finds himself
in Roman custody. That same night
Paul has a religious experience
in which he hears a voice say:

"Don't be afraid!
You have given your witness for me
here in Jerusalem, and you must also
do the same in Rome." ACTS 23:11

The next morning Paul's enemies
take an oath not to eat or drink
until they have killed him.
Paul's nephew hears about the plot
and warns his uncle (ACTS 23:16).
Paul alerts the commander,
who removes him to a distant jail
in Caesarea-on-the-Sea.

What are my thoughts
as I imagine myself to be Paul
and reflect upon the Lord's words,
"Don't be afraid"?

The life of Felix, governor of Caesarea,
reads like bad movie script.
Born a slave, he was freed by the emperor,
married the granddaughter
of Mark Antony and Cleopatra, and
became the first slave in Roman history
to become a provincial governor.

Ancient historians
paint an ugly picture of Felix:

Tacitus says
even when ruling a province,
Felix did it "in the spirit of a slave." . . .
He accepted bribes wherever and
whenever he could get them.

BENJAMIN WILLARD ROBINSON, *The Life of Paul*

It is to this man that Paul's opponents
send a delegation when they hear
of Paul's removal to Caesarea.

Felix listens to the delegation
and then invites Paul to respond.
Paul says fearlessly:

"As you can find out for yourself,
it was no more than twelve days ago
that I went to Jerusalem to worship.
The Jews did not find me arguing
with anyone in the Temple, nor did
they find me stirring up the people. . . .

Suggested reading: Acts 24:10–27

I do admit . . .
I worship the God of our ancestors
by following that Way [Christianity]
which they say is false." ACTS 24:11–12, 14

After hearing Paul's side of the story,
Felix delays any immediate decision.
A few days later, he sends for Paul,
presumably to talk about Jesus.
But he has other motives. Luke says:

[Felix] was hoping
that Paul would give him some money;
and for this reason he would call
for him often and talk with him. ACTS 24:26

Paul refuses to play Felix's game
and pays dearly for it: He is warehoused
in prison for the next two years.

All this time, Paul's heart cries out
for freedom to preach the Good News
to the masses beyond Caesarea.
But for the present,
he can only pray, dream, and hope.

What are my thoughts
as I imagine myself to be Paul
and try to figure out
why God is letting my life
take such a tragic turn?

Dietrich Bonhoeffer was
a Lutheran pastor and theologian.
He openly opposed the Nazis
during World War II.

Eventually they seized him.
Like Paul, he spent two years in prison.
Also like Paul, he used his time to write.
The following excerpts
from his "Night Voices in Tegel"
preserve for us some of his thoughts
prior to his execution on April 9, 1945:

Stretched out on my cot
I stare at the grey wall.
Outside, a summer evening
That does not know me
Goes singing into the countryside. . . .

Night and silence. . . .

I hear my own soul tremble and heave. . . .
I hear the uneasy creak of the beds. . . .
I hear how sleepless men toss and turn,
Who long for freedom. . . .

Night and silence. . . .

Brother, till the night be past,
Pray for me!

Paul experiences similar nights
of endless tossing and turning

in his prison cell in Caesarea.
Then one night his hopes soar briefly.
Festus replaces Felix as governor.
But as quickly as Paul's hopes soar
they crash.

Paul's enemies get to Festus first
and persuade him
to return Paul to Jerusalem for trial.

Paul fears that
he can never get justice in Jerusalem.
So he asks to be tried in Rome.

All Roman citizens had a right
to appeal their case to the emperor.
A law from Octavian's time stated
that if citizens living outside Rome
had misgivings about getting justice
in a provincial court,
they could have their case heard in Rome.

This is what Paul, a Roman citizen,
now requests and gets.

What are my thoughts as I try
to understand why God lets good people,
like Bonhoeffer and Paul,
suffer injustices
at the hands of evil people?

Five British explorers froze to death
in 1912 during a polar expedition.
A passage from the journal
of one of them sounds like something
that Paul might have written
as he set out for Rome:

So I live,
knowing that I am in God's hands,
to be used to bring others to him . . .
or to die tomorrow if he so wills. . . .

We must do what we can
and leave the rest to him. . . .
My trust is in God
so that it matters not
what I do or where I go. EDWARD WILSON

Just as one of the explorers
kept a journal of the British expedition,
so Luke kept a journal of Paul's Roman trip.
It is found in the Acts of the Apostles
and is written in the first person (ACTS 27–28).

Paul was just one of many prisoners
being taken to Rome under guard.
Probably a number of them
had already been condemned to death
and were scheduled to die in the arena.

Luke, who accompanied Paul to Rome,
probably signed on

as Paul's personal servant (ACTS 19:29).
An ancient letter of Pliny testifies
that Roman citizens had a right
to servants, even in custody.

Before the voyage reached
its midpoint, a great storm blew up.
It became so violent the captain ordered
cargo thrown overboard.
Luke writes:

*For many days we could not
see the sun or the stars,
and the wind kept on blowing.* ACTS 27:20

Then one night the ship blows into
dangerous waters. The situation is bad.

*Before dawn . . . Paul took some bread,
gave thanks to God before them all,
broke it, and began to eat.
They took courage, and
every one of them also ate some food.
After everyone had eaten enough,
they lightened the ship by throwing
all the wheat [cargo] into the sea.*
ACTS 27:33, 35–36, 38

*How do I interpret
Paul's predawn action of taking bread,
giving thanks, breaking it, and eating it?*

When day came,
the sailors did not recognize the coast,
but they noticed a bay with a beach
and decided that, if possible,
they would run the ship aground there. . . .

But the ship hit a sandbank and . . .
the back part was being broken to pieces
by the violence of the waves. . . .

[An officer] ordered everyone
who could swim to jump overboard first
and swim ashore;
the rest were to follow,
holding on to the planks
or to some broken pieces of the ship.
And this was how
we all got safely to shore. ACTS 27:39, 41, 43–44

The shipwrecked crew was fortunate
to have landed on friendly Malta.
There were other shores
where they would have been killed.

The crew and passengers rest
for an extended period on the island.

When suitable sailing weather returns,
they resume their voyage to Rome
on a ship called *The Twin Gods*.
Eventually the ship reaches
the port of Puteoli on the Italian coast.

From there, the soldiers
march the prisoners on foot to Rome.
Luke writes of the march:

The believers in Rome
heard about us and came
as far as the towns of Market of Appius
and Three Inns to meet us.

When Paul saw them,
he thanked God
and was greatly encouraged.

When we arrived in Rome,
Paul was allowed to live by himself
with a soldier guarding him. ACTS 28:15–16

In other words,
Paul is put under an ancient form
of house arrest.
This gives him considerable freedom
and is a welcome relief from
his former imprisonment in Caesarea.

What are my thoughts
as I imagine myself to be Paul
and see the Christians of Rome
coming out to meet me?
What are my thoughts
when I see the city of Rome itself?

Once Paul got settled, around 61 C.E.,
he met with local Jewish leaders.
They were eager to talk with him, saying:

*"We would like to hear your ideas,
because we know that everywhere
people speak against this party
to which you belong."* ACTS 28:22

Paul welcomes the opportunity
to talk about "this party" (Christianity).

*From morning till night
he explained to them his message
about the Kingdom of God, and
he tried to convince them about Jesus
by quoting from the Law of Moses
and the writings of the prophets.
Some of them were convinced . . .
but others would not believe.
So they left, disagreeing.* ACTS 28:23–25

The Acts of the Apostles ends, saying:

*For two years Paul . . .
welcomed all who came to see him.
He preached about the Kingdom of God
and taught about the Lord Jesus Christ,
speaking with all boldness and freedom.*
ACTS 28:30–31

Luke never does tell us what happened
at Paul's trial in Rome.

One of Paul's own letters suggests
that he was freed (2 TIMOTHY 4:16–17).

Perhaps he then went to Spain (ROMANS 15:24),
Asia Minor (TITUS 3:12),
Macedonia (1 TIMOTHY 1:3), and Crete (TITUS 1:5).

Once back in Rome,
Paul appears to have been brought
to trial again.
This time he is convicted (2 TIMOTHY 4:6).
Tradition says he was beheaded
in Rome around 67 C.E.

And so the question returns:
Why did Luke leave Acts unfinished?

One answer is
that Luke left it unfinished on purpose,
because its story is still unfinished.
The preaching of the Good News
goes on—and must go on—
until the world is fully re-created
and Jesus returns in all his glory.

*What am I doing to help complete
the last chapter of Acts?
How might I contribute more concretely
to the preaching of the Good News and
to the re-creation of our world?*

299

What did Paul look like?
What kind of speaker was he?
Why was he able to touch so profoundly
the lives and hearts of so many people?

There are clues in Paul's letters
that suggest that he was neither
an impressive-looking person
nor a dynamic speaker.
For example,
Paul writes to the Christians in Corinth:

I, Paul, make a personal appeal to you—
I who am said to be meek and mild
when I am with you,
but harsh with you when I am away.
By the gentleness and kindness of Christ
I beg you not to force me to be harsh
when I come. 2 CORINTHIANS 10:1–2

Further on in the same letter,
Paul writes:

Someone will say,
"Paul's letters are severe and strong,
but when he is with us in person,
he is weak, and his words are nothing!"
2 CORINTHIANS 10:10

Both of these statements suggest
that Paul was unimpressive both
as a person and as a speaker.

How, then,
do we account for Paul's impact on people?
Why did his opponents fear him so much?
Again, Paul suggests the answer himself.
In another letter to the Corinthians
he writes:

My teaching
and message were not delivered
with skillful words of human wisdom,
but with convincing proof of the power
of God's Spirit.
Your faith, then, does not rest on
human wisdom but on God's power.

1 CORINTHIANS 2:4–5

The key to Paul's power over people
was not his own skill or eloquence,
but the power of the Holy Spirit
working through him.

I pray in a low, audible voice
the following prayer, pausing after each
sentence to reflect upon it
and to speak to the Spirit about it.
"O come, O Holy Spirit, come!
Come as holy light and lead us.
Come as holy truth and teach us.
Come as holy power and strengthen us."

ANCIENT PRAYER (Adapted)

9 World of Early Church _____

Weeks

Timeline (key dates, traditional—C.E.)

c. 33	Pentecost
	Jerusalem ministry
	Jerusalem persecution
45	Global ministry
64	Nero's persecution
67	Paul's death
81–96	Domitian's reign

Bible (key books)

1–2 Thessalonians	Titus
Galatians	1–2 Timothy
Philippians	Hebrews
1–2 Corinthians	James
Romans	1–2 Peter
Philemon	1–2–3 John
Colossians	Jude
Ephesians	Revelation

MACEDONIA

• Philippi

Thessalonica •

Berea •

• Troas

ASIA MINOR

GALATIA

Athens •

Ephesus •

• Iconium

• Lystra

• Colossae

• Derbe

• Tarsus

Corinth •

• Antioch

CRETE

CYPRUS

SYRIA

MEDITERRANEAN
SEA

• Damascus

JUDEA

Jerusalem •

EGYPT

Tradition attributes thirteen letters
to Paul and groups them as follows:

Early: 1–2 Thessalonians
Great: 1–2 Corinthians,
            Galatians, Romans
Prison: Philippians, Colossians,
            Ephesians, Philemon
Pastoral: 1–2 Timothy, Titus

Paul wrote his first letter to the
Thessalonians about 50 C.E., after learning
they thought Jesus was going to return
shortly and take them *alive* into heaven.

When some Thessalonians died,
their families were deeply saddened,
thinking these family members
would never see Jesus or be with God.
Paul sent them a letter
to clear up their confusion. He wrote:

From Paul, Silas, and Timothy—
To the people of the church
in Thessalonica, who belong to God
the Father and the Lord Jesus Christ:
May grace and peace be yours.

We always thank God for you. . . .
We want you to know the truth
about those who have died. . . .
Jesus died and rose again, and . . .

*God will take back with Jesus
those who have died believing in him. . . .*

*There is no need to write you . . .
about the times and occasions. . . .
The Day of the Lord will come as a thief
comes at night . . .*

*Read this letter to all the believers.
The grace of our Lord Jesus Christ be with
you.* 1 THESSALONIANS 1:1–2; 4:13–14; 5:1–2, 27–28

Paul follows up his first letter
with a second one, which clarifies
some questions related to
the Second Coming. 2 THESSALONIANS 2:1–10

Paul's two letters illustrate
the general format that he follows
in most of his correspondence:

- *salutation,* containing the sender's
  name, receiver's name, and a greeting;
- *thanksgiving,* acting as a bridge
  to the body of the letter;
- *body of the letter;*
- *conclusion,* containing
  a personal comment and a blessing.

*Some fundamentalists think Jesus' final
coming is near. Why do/don't I agree?*

Sydney Piddington was a teenager
when he was captured in World War II.
He was imprisoned in Singapore
with other Australian POWs.
One thing that helped him survive was
Lin Yutang's book *The Importance of Living*.
It is a book that you don't simply read.
Rather, you meditate on it.

The kind of "meditative" reading
that Piddington found in Lin Yutang's book
is also found in Paul's *great* letters
(1–2 Corinthians, Galatians, and Romans).

Take his First Letter to the Corinthians.

Ancient plays portrayed Corinthians
as drunks, perverts, and rowdies.
Paul's first Letter reflects that image.
Writing from Ephesus in 57 C.E., he says:

Few of you were wise or powerful
or of high social standing.
God purposely chose
what the world considers nonsense
in order to shame the wise.
1 CORINTHIANS 1:26

It is understandable, therefore,
that some Corinthians occasionally
slipped back into their old ways.
Referring to this, Paul writes:

306

Now, it is actually being said that
there is sexual immorality among you
so terrible that not even the heathen
would be guilty of it. . . .
Don't you know that your body
is the temple of the Holy Spirit . . . ?
So use your bodies for God's glory.

1 CORINTHIANS 5:1, 6:19–20

Later, Paul discusses "divisions"
that are threatening the Corinthian flock.
To illustrate the kind of unity
that should exist among them,
Paul uses this striking image:

Christ is like a single body,
which has many parts;
it is still one body, even though
it is made up of different parts.
In the same way, all of us . . .
are Christ's body. . . .
It is love, then, that you should
strive for. 1 CORINTHIANS 12:12–13, 27; 14:1

"I may give away everything I have,
and even give up my body to be burned—
but if I have no love, this does me no good."

1 CORINTHIANS 13:3

How do I strive to grow in love and
in unity with Christ's body, the Church?

307

"They are chopping me up!"
That's what a minister told a friend
after losing both legs
to injuries received on a battlefield.
Unable to continue his normal ministry,
he felt "trapped . . . in his wheelchair."
Then one day a doctor asked him
to minister to patients in tragic situations
similar to his own.

Suddenly he found himself
helping people who needed him far more
than his former parishioners did.
Now, for the first time, he understood
the meaning of this passage in
Paul's Second Letter to the Corinthians:

The God and Father
of our Lord Jesus Christ . . .
helps us in our troubles,
so that we are able to help others . . .
using the same help that we ourselves
have received from God. 2 CORINTHIANS 1:3–4

Later, Paul asks Christians
who have moved from poverty to wealth
to minister to their brothers and sisters
who are in need, saying:

You should each give, then,
as you have decided,

not with regret or out of a sense of duty;
for God loves the one who gives gladly.
2 CORINTHIANS 9:7

Paul ends his letter,
sharing with his readers how the Lord
helped him with a personal problem:

Three times I prayed to the Lord
about this and asked him to take it away.
But his answer was:
"My grace is all you need,
for my power is greatest
when you are weak."

I am most happy, then,
to be proud of my weaknesses,
in order to feel
the protection of Christ's power over me.
I am content with weaknesses . . .
and difficulties for Christ's sake.
For when I am weak, then I am strong.
2 CORINTHIANS 12:8–10

How honestly and confidently can I pray
these faith-filled words of Paul:
"I have learned this secret,
so that anywhere, at any time, . . .
I have the strength to face all conditions
by the power that Christ gives me"?
PHILIPPIANS 4:12–13

Leopold Stokowski was conducting
the Philadelphia orchestra.
One overture featured a trumpet,
played offstage.
Twice the time came for it to sound;
twice it didn't sound.

After the overture Stokowski stormed
offstage to find the trumpet player.
There he was—arms pinned to his sides
by a burly security guard, who said,
"This nut was trying to play his horn
while your concert was going on."

As the "well-meaning" guard frustrated
Stokowski's overture, so well-meaning
people were frustrating Paul's work.
Jewish converts to Christianity
were telling Gentile converts in Galatia
that they had to be circumcised.

When Paul heard about this,
he wrote a letter to the Galatians,
telling them, in effect:
"Think of Judaism and circumcision
as the scaffolding of a building.
Think of Christ and his Body, the Church,
as the building.
Once the building is erected in place,
the scaffolding is no longer needed."
Paul concludes:

*It does not matter at all
whether or not one is circumcised;
what does matter
is being a new creature.* GALATIANS 6:15

This brings us to Paul's last *great* letter:
the Letter to the Romans.
Written around 58 C.E. from Corinth,
it reviews how Jesus fulfills
the prophecies and is the son of David
and the Son of God (ROMANS 1:2–4).

It goes on to say that because
we are baptized into Christ, we should
have nothing to do with sin (ROMANS 6).
Paul is quick to add
that this does not mean
we will not feel an attraction to sin.
Paul himself felt this (ROMANS 7:15–24).
It means that baptism empowers us
to defeat sin and suffering. Paul ends:

*If we share Christ's suffering,
we will also share his glory. . . .
What we suffer . . .
cannot be compared at all with the glory
that is going to be revealed.* ROMANS 8:17–18

*What motivates me most
to continue the never-ending battle
to defeat sin and suffering?*

311

A modern peace activist was jailed
for hammering, in *symbolic* protest,
on an F15 bomber. (It costs $40 million
and burns $6,000 worth of fuel a minute
while in flight.) He wrote in a letter:

The jail we are currently in is awful. . . .
The TV blares at full volume all day
and all night. We have no privacy.
We are led around in chains and shackles.
Our mail is censored; much of it
is turned away. We are allowed
no books. . . . I have not been outdoors
in over a month. JOHN DEAR, S.J.

Paul could relate to this *prison* letter.
He wrote four letters from prison:
Philippians (1:7), Colossians (4:10),
Philemon (23), and Ephesians (6:20).

Paul's Letter to the Philippians contains
this beautiful meditation on Jesus,
the eternal Son of the eternal Father,
who took flesh, died, rose, ascended,
and now reigns over all creation.

[Jesus] always had the nature of God,
but . . . took the nature of a servant . . .
and walked the path of obedience
all the way to death—
his death on the cross.

*For this reason God . . . gave him the name
that is greater than any other name.
And so, in honor of the name of Jesus
all . . . will fall on their knees,
and all will openly proclaim
that Jesus Christ is Lord.* PHILIPPIANS 2:6–11

This brings us to Paul's second *prison*
letter: Letter to the Colossians.
It, too, contains a beautiful meditation
that focuses on
Jesus' role in God's plan, in general, and
Jesus' role in the Church, in particular:

*Christ is the visible likeness
of the invisible God.
He is the first-born Son,
superior to all created things. . . .
He is the head of his body, the church;
he is the source of the body's life.
He is the first-born Son,
who was raised from death, in order that
he alone might have the first place
in all things.* COLOSSIANS 1:15, 18

*How do I understand these words
of Louis Evely: "Christ is just as much
the revelation of ourselves
as he is the revelation of God"?
What is at least one example of this?*

Onesimus was a runaway slave
whom Paul instructed and baptized.
Onesimus was the property
of a new Christian named Philemon.
Paul wrote his third *prison* letter
to Philemon. He says:

I am sending Onesimus back to you now,
and with him goes my heart.
He is not just a slave,
but . . . a dear brother in Christ.
Welcome him back,
just as you would welcome me.
If he has done you any wrong
or owes you anything,
charge it to my account. . . .
I will write this with my own hand:
I, Paul, will pay you back. PHILEMON 12, 16–19

Few letters reveal the warmth of Paul
as does this Letter to Philemon.

It brings us to Paul's last *prison* letter,
Letter to the Ephesians.
Its style and theology are so distinctive
that some suggest it is the work
of one of Paul's later disciples.
But such speculation is often pointless.
Besides, like many ancients, Paul
dictated his letters in general terms
and then signed the finished version.

With my own hand I write this:
Greetings from Paul.
This is the way I sign every letter;
this is how I write. 2 THESSALONIANS 3:17

The Letter to the Ephesians contains
a beautiful summary of God's plan
to "re-create" the world.

[It] is to bring all creation together,
everything in heaven and earth,
with Christ as head. . . . God chose us . . .
in our union with Christ. . . .
[God] appointed some to be apostles,
others to be prophets, . . . evangelists, . . .
pastors and teachers.
[God] did this to prepare all God's people
for the work of Christian service,
in order to build up the body of Christ.
                     EPHESIANS 1:10–11, 4:11–12

And so God has called us in Jesus
and empowered us through the Spirit
to play a role in building up Christ's body
on earth, the Church.

"Before God can do his thing,
I must do my thing." SAINT AUGUSTINE (Adapted)
What is my thing, regarding the Gospel?

315

The paintings of artists often reflect
a growth in their aesthetic understanding.
Paul's letters reflect a similar growth
in his theological understanding.
This is so clear in his *pastoral* letters
that scholars theorize they were written
by a disciple of Paul at a later date—
perhaps after Paul died in 67 C.E.

Theorizing aside, tradition attributes
three *pastoral* letters to Paul:
two letters to Timothy and one to Titus.

The First Letter to Timothy
reflects a Christian community
that is beginning to organize itself.
It treats such topics as qualifications
for church leaders and church helpers.

*A church leader . . . must be able
to manage his own family well and . . .
be mature in the faith. . . . Church helpers
must . . . [be] able to speak boldly about
their faith in Jesus Christ.* 1 TIMOTHY 3:2, 4, 6, 8, 13

The Second Letter to Timothy
contains this beautiful passage:

*All Scripture is inspired by God
and is useful for teaching the truth,
rebuking error, correcting faults,
and giving instruction for right living.*

*The time will come when people will not
listen to sound doctrine, but will
follow . . . teachers who will tell them
what they are itching to hear.*
2 TIMOTHY 3:16, 4:3

The final *pastoral* letter is to Titus.
Like Timothy, Titus was Paul's coworker.
The Letter to Titus also reflects
a community that is organizing itself.
It refers to the fact that Timothy
stayed on in Crete for a while to do
what "needed doing" and to "appoint
church elders in every town" (TITUS 1:5).

The letter also discusses qualifications
for church leaders.
They must be "self-controlled, upright,
holy, and disciplined" (TITUS 1:8).
The letter concludes
with this pastoral advice to Titus:

*Show a gentle attitude toward everyone.
For we ourselves were once . . . slaves
to passions and pleasures.* TITUS 3:2–3

*Which of Paul's above instructions
to Titus or Timothy is especially
relevant for today's Church? Why?*

A military plane carrying 30,000 letters
crashed off the coast of Newfoundland.
At considerable risk to their lives,
divers recovered the canvas mailbags.

Why the concern for these letters?
Experience shows that soldiers
cope better with food shortages
than they do with letter shortages.

The leaders of the early Church
also knew the importance of letters.
They used them to keep in touch
with distant brothers and sisters.

Besides the thirteen letters
traditionally attributed to Paul,
there are eight other letters.
Seven of these are often referred to
as general ("catholic") letters,
so-called because they are addressed
to no particular church. These are:

James   1–2–3 John
1–2 Peter   Jude

The eighth and final letter is Hebrews.
Unlike the previous seven letters,
it makes no reference to its author.
This has sparked a "guessing game"
about who wrote it.

Here we need to remember something
about ancient authorship
that applies equally to biblical authorship.
It is often attributed to someone
who commissions or approves it.

*[And so] an apostle's name attached
to a book may indicate no more than
that he gave it his approval or simply
that it is the written form of his
personal teaching.* RODERICK A. F. MACKENZIE

As we know, this practice is also followed
in many instances in modern times.
The president of the United States
rarely writes his official documents.
The president merely approves
what another writes under his direction.
The pope and other leaders do the same.

The important thing is not *who* wrote
the biblical writings, but *what* God intends
to teach us through them.

*How do I understand
the following quotation from Martin Luther?
"The Bible is alive, it speaks to me;
it has feet, it runs after me;
it has hands, it lays hold of me."*

The Teahouse of the August Moon
is a play set on the island of Okinawa.
It opens with Sakini,
an interpreter for the American army,
walking down to the footlights
and introducing himself to the audience.

After describing how Okinawa
has been conquered many, many times,
he notes that this has helped to educate
his people. Then he adds reflectively:

*Not easy to learn. Sometimes painful.
But pain makes man think.
Thought makes man wise.
Wisdom makes life endurable.*

This same "wisdom" approach to life
permeates the Letter from James.
It treats such practical topics as

* persevering under trial   (1:2–18),
* avoiding discrimination   (2:1–13),
* helping the poor   (5:1–6).

The letter's style and tone are more
like those of a sermon than of a letter,
suggesting it may have been a sermon
that was converted into a letter.
One passage, especially, deserves note.
It discusses the relationship between
faith and action. It reads:

What good is it
for one of you to say that you have faith
if your actions do not prove it?
Can that faith save you?

Suppose there are brothers or sisters
who need clothes
and don't have enough to eat.
What good is there in your saying
to them, "God bless you!
Keep warm and eat well!"—
if you don't give them
the necessities of life?

So it is with faith; if it is alone and
includes no actions, then it is dead.
JAMES 2:14–17

There is no better summary of this
passage than Saint Paul's famous words:

I may have all the faith needed
to move mountains—but if I have no love,
I am nothing. 1 CORINTHIANS 13:2

"Happiness will never be ours
if we do not recognize to some degree
that God's blessings were given us
for the well-being of all." ANONYMOUS
What are some of God's blessings to me?

During World War II,
Father Titus Brandsma died
in a Nazi concentration camp.
He left behind a tattered prayer book.
The Nazis failed to notice
that between its lines of print
Father Brandsma had written the story
of his prison sufferings.

There, too,
he penned this poetic piece
that describes the spiritual impact
that the experience had on him:

No grief shall fall my way, but I
Shall see Thy grief-filled eyes;
The lonely way that Thou once walked
Has made me sorrow-wise. . . .

Stay with me, Jesus, only stay;
I shall not fear
If, reaching out my hand,
I feel Thee near.

KILIAN J. HEALY, *Walking with God*

The people for which
the First Letter of Peter was intended
would have appreciated these lines.
They, too, were suffering immensely.
Probably written around 64 C.E.,
the letter seeks to bolster their spirits
by reminding them:

*Christ himself suffered for you
and left you an example,
so that you would follow in his steps.*
1 PETER 2:21

The cause of their suffering isn't given,
but it may be inferred from
what is said elsewhere in the letter:

*The heathen are surprised
when you do not join them
in the same wild and reckless living,
and so they insult you. . . .
Happy are you if you are insulted
because you are Christ's followers.*
1 PETER 4:4, 14

*"Not until each loom is silent
And the shuttles cease to fly,
Will God unroll the pattern
And explain the reason why.
The dark threads are as needful
In the weaver's skillful hand
As the threads of gold and silver
for the pattern which is planned."*
AUTHOR UNKNOWN

*If someone told me that
he or she could no longer believe in God
because of all the suffering in the world,
what might I say to that person?*

Time affects our perception of reality,
whether it be the Vietnam War
or the Civil Rights Movement.
Time has a way of producing
a change or a different slant on things.

This happened in biblical times.
Some people began to modify and change
the things Jesus had said and done.

Referring to these people,
Peter laments that they have strayed
from the flock and have become lost.
He goes so far as to say:

*It would have been much better
for them never to have known
the way of righteousness than to know it
and then turn away from
the sacred command that was given them.*

2 PETER 2:21

One teaching from which some people
were turning away
was the Second Coming of Jesus.
They expected Jesus to come quickly.
When Jesus didn't come,
they began to question if he'd come at all.

2 Peter addresses this critical issue.
It reminds its readers
that in God's sight there is no difference.

Between one day and a thousand years;
to him the two are the same. 2 PETER 3:8

Reassuring its readers,
the letter refers to Matthew 16:5, saying:

We have not depended on made-up stories
in making known to you the mighty
coming of our Lord Jesus Christ.
With our own eyes we saw his greatness.

We were there when he was given
honor and glory by God the Father,
when the voice came to him
from the Supreme Glory, saying,

"This is my own dear Son,
with whom I am pleased!"
We ourselves heard this voice coming
from heaven, when we were with him
on the holy mountain. 2 PETER 1:16–18

"The shadow on the dial,
the striking of the clock . . .
these are
the arbitrary and outward signs,
the measure of time, but not time itself.
Time is the life of the soul."

HENRY WADSWORTH LONGFELLOW

How do I tend to view time? Eternity?

325

John's first and most important letter
warns his readers against false teachers.
He refers to them, collectively, as the
"Enemy of Christ," or the "Antichrist"
(as some Bibles translate it), saying:

Those who say that Jesus is not the Messiah . . .
are the Enemy of Christ. . . .
Do not believe all who claim to have
the Spirit, but test them to find out if
the spirit they have comes from God. . . .
Anyone who acknowledges that
Jesus Christ came as a human being
has the Spirit. . . .
Anyone who denies this about Jesus
does not. . . . The spirit that he has
is from the Enemy of Christ. 1 JOHN 2:22, 4:1–3

One group of false teachers are *Docetists*.
They teach that Jesus only "appeared"
to have a human body, and, therefore,
he was not a true human being.

A second set are the *Gnostics*.
They teach that all matter is evil, and,
therefore, Jesus is neither the Son of God
nor the Messiah, because neither of them
would be joined to something evil.

Thus these two sets of false teachers
deny Jesus to be:

- a human being   (1 JOHN 4:2),
- the Messiah   (1 JOHN 2:22),
- the Son of God   (1 JOHN 2:23).

John affirms Jesus' humanity and divinity:

We write to you about the Word of life,
which has existed from the very beginning.
We have heard it,
and we have seen it with our eyes. . . .
What we have seen and heard
we announce to you also, so that you
will join with us in the fellowship
that we have with the Father and
with his Son Jesus Christ. 1 JOHN 1:1–3

John's second letter is only a note,
addressed to "the dear Lady and
to her children" (a church in Asia Minor).
It exhorts them to love one another and
to guard against false teachers.

The final letter is also a mere note.
It is addressed to Gaius and warns the
local church about a local church leader
who has broken with John and
is trying to lead the community astray.

Jesus is truly human, the Messiah,
and the Son of God. To which of these
do I relate with the deepest faith? Why?

One of Jesus' parables
concerns a farmer who planted a field.
An enemy oversowed it with weeds.
When the farmer's hired hands
saw the weeds, they asked the farmer
if they should uproot them.

"No," he answered,
"because as you gather the weeds
you might pull up some of the wheat. . . .
Let . . . both grow together until harvest.
Then I will tell the harvest workers
to pull up the weeds first,
tie them in bundles and burn them,
and then to gather in the wheat
and put it in my barn." MATTHEW 13:29–30

Jude's letter addresses a situation
similar to the one in Jesus' parable.
Of special note is Jude's observation
that some "godless people"
are distorting the message of Jesus
"to excuse their immoral ways" (JUDE 4).

Jude's point is a good one.
He is saying
that when belief and behavior clash,
we can become a Dr. Jekyll and Mr. Hyde.
We can split down the middle,
believing one way
and behaving in a totally different way.

Since living this way is uncomfortable,
we try to resolve our conflict.

First, we usually try
to change our behavior to fit our belief.
If we cannot do this,
we change our belief to fit our behavior.

The "godless people" chose the latter path.
Jude says of them:

They are like wild waves of the sea,
with their shameful deeds
showing up like foam.
They are like wandering stars,
for whom God
has reserved a place forever
in the deepest darkness. JUDE 13

Jude ends his letter, telling his readers:

Pray in the power of the Holy Spirit,
and keep yourselves in the love of God,
as you wait
for our Lord Jesus Christ in his mercy
to give you eternal life. JUDE 20–21

What would I tell someone
who is split down the middle:
believing in one way
but behaving another—unable to change?

Author Ardis Whitman writes:

When I was eight
I went to a circus in Boston
and marveled at the trapeze artists,
soaring impossibly through space,
always catching
the flying swing from each other.
"Aren't they scared?"
I whispered to my mother.
A man in the row ahead turned to answer,
"They aren't scared, honey," he said gently.
"They trust each other." "The Courage to Trust"

The Letter to the Hebrews
is a impassioned call to trust Jesus.
The Jewish converts to whom
it is penned are suffering
from some trials and are tempted
to turn their backs on Jesus.
The letter exhorts them:

[Keep your] eyes fixed on Jesus. . . .
Think of what he went through;
how he put up with
so much hatred from sinners!
So do not let yourselves
become discouraged. HEBREWS 12:2–3

The letter exhorts the Jewish converts
to imitate their ancestors, saying:

*It was faith that made Abraham
able to become a father,
even though he was too old. . . .
It was faith that made Abraham
offer his son Isaac as a sacrifice. . . .
It was faith that made Moses . . .
suffer with God's people.*
HEBREWS 11:11, 17, 24–25

The suffering of the Jewish converts
recalls Jesus' warning to his disciples:

*"If people persecuted me, . . .
they will persecute you too."* JOHN 15:20

The letter assures its readers
that Jesus understands their struggle:

*Our High Priest
is not one who cannot feel sympathy
for our weaknesses. . . .
We have a High Priest who was tempted
in every way that we are, but did not sin.*
HEBREWS 4:15

*"Be glad . . .
of the many kinds of trials you suffer.
Their purpose is to prove
that your faith is genuine."* 1 PETER 1:6–7
What is one trial I have suffered?

331

Persistence of Memory
is an eerie painting by Salvadore Dali.
Against a stark backdrop, three watches,
looking like slices of melted cheese,
drape over weird objects.
Pondering Dali's surrealistic creation
is like pondering a scene from a dream.

We get a similar impression
when we ponder the Book of Revelation.
It is filled with dreamlike images
granted to "John" during visions
on Patmos, an island in the Aegean Sea.
Civil authorities had banished John
to the island for preaching about Jesus.

John's experience began
on the Lord's Day, when he heard a voice.
Turning around, he saw Jesus
standing amid seven lamp stands—
symbolizing seven churches
(Ephesus, Smyrna, Pergamum, Thyatira,
Sardis, Philadelphia, and Laodicea).

All seven churches
were facing persecution under Domitian,
the current Roman emperor (81–96 C.E.).

At the sight of Jesus,
John fell to the ground "like a dead man."
But Jesus reached down, touched him,

and said, "Don't be afraid!" (REVELATION 1:17).
Then Jesus dictated seven messages
to John, one for each threatened church.

The messages commend the churches
on some points and correct them on others.
The general theme of the messages
is summed up in this excerpt to the church
of Smyrna (in modern Turkey):

"This is the message from the one . . .
who died and lived again. . . .
The Devil will put you to the test. . . .
Be faithful to me, . . .
and I will give you life
as your prize of victory." REVELATION 2:8, 10

After the dictation is completed,
the visions begin to unfold,
somewhat like a stage play in three acts:

Act 1: *Preview visions* (REVELATION 4:1–8:5)—
seven seals
Act 2: *Conflict visions* (REVELATION 8:6–15:8)—
seven trumpets, dragon, beasts
Act 3: *Judgment visions* (REVELATION 16:1ff.)—
seven bowls, Babylon, Jerusalem

What are my thoughts as I imagine
I am John, writing down the above excerpt
to the church of Smyrna?

"Act 1" opens with a heavenly voice
telling John, "Come up here, and I will show
you what must happen" (REVELATION 4:1).

John sees God on a throne, holding a scroll
with seven seals. John weeps, because
no one can be found who is worthy
to take the scroll and break its seals.
Then a Lamb appears—he is worthy!
The Lamb breaks the first four seals.
They reveal:

- a white horse, whose rider
  wears a crown, previewing *victory;*
- a red horse, whose rider carries
  a sword, previewing *conflict*
  between the forces of good and evil;
- a black horse, whose rider carries
  a scale, previewing *judgment* (evil),
  reward (good), and punishment; and
- a pale green horse, whose rider
  is named Death and Hades,
  previewing the *fate of the evil forces.*

Then the Lamb breaks the *fifth* seal.
It reveals a host of martyred Christians,
who are told more will join them soon.
Next the Lamb breaks the *sixth* seal,
revealing cosmic catastrophes that
cause people to shout to the mountains:
"Hide us" (REVELATION 6:16).

After this, four angels come from
the four corners of the earth to mark
the foreheads of the 144,000 people.
(This symbolic number derives from the
12,000 in each of Israel's twelve tribes
and previews those who will remain faithful
to Jesus, the "new Israel.")
"Dressed in white robes and holding palm
branches," they have "washed their robes
and made them white with the blood
of the Lamb" (REVELATION 7:9, 14).

Then the Lamb breaks the *seventh* seal,
and silence fills heaven (REVELATION 8:1).

It is a solemn moment.
The *preview* visions begin to fade;
the hour of *conflict* is at hand.

Seven angels receive seven trumpets.
An eighth angel places on an altar
a container of prayers
and then hurls fire down to earth.
The fire triggers thunder, lightning,
catastrophes, and earthquakes.

The curtain falls; it is the end of "Act 1."

*What are my thoughts
as I imagine myself to be John
and ponder the "preview visions"?*

"Act 2" (the *conflict* visions)
takes place in two dramatic "scenes"
and describes the battle
between the forces of good and evil.

The first scene begins
with seven angels sounding, in order,
the seven trumpets.
They unleash a series of plagues
not unlike those of ancient Egypt.
And like the ancient Egyptians,
the evil forces on earth remain obstinate.

When the *seventh* trumpet sounds,
a chorus of heavenly voices cries out:

*"The power to rule over the world
belongs now to our Lord
and his Messiah. . . .
The time has come to destroy those
who destroy the earth!"* REVELATION 11:15, 18

Then a mysterious woman,
dressed in the sun, appears in the sky
and gives birth to a son.
A dragon sees the son and tries to kill it.
But, like Jesus,
who was saved at birth from Herod,
the child is also snatched to safety.

Then war breaks out in heaven
between "the dragon" and "his angels"

and "Michael" and "his angels"
(REVELATION 12:7).
Michael's forces defeat the dragon's
and hurls them to earth.
There, they immediately begin to pursue
the woman's descendants:
the followers of Jesus (REVELATION 12:17).

Meanwhile, a beast leaps from the sea
and receives power from the dragon.
All the people except the faithful worship it—
until it is wounded.

Then a second beast
breathes life back into the first beast,
whose number is 666 (REVELATION 13:18).
(This is the numerical sum of the letters
of the name of Nero,
the first Roman emperor
to persecute the Christians of Rome.
It suggests
that the second beast is Domitian.)

Then the curtain falls
on the first scene of "Act 2."

*What are my thoughts
as I imagine myself to be John
and prayerfully ponder all of this?*

The second scene of "Act 2"
shifts the focus from
the dragon and the unfaithful
to the Lamb and the faithful. John says:

*Then I looked, and there was the Lamb
standing on Mount Zion;
with him were 144,000 people
who have his name and his Father's name
written on their foreheads. . . .
The 144,000 people
stood before the throne . . .
singing a new song,
which only they could learn.
Of the whole human race
they are the only ones
who have been redeemed. . . .
They follow the Lamb wherever he goes. . . .*

*Then I saw another angel
flying high in the air,
with an eternal message of Good News
to announce to the peoples
of the earth. . . .
He said in a loud voice,
"Honor God and praise his greatness!
For the time has come for him
to judge all people.
Worship him who made heaven,
earth, sea, and the springs of water!" . . .*

Then I looked,
and there was a white cloud,
and sitting on the cloud
was what looked like a human being,
with a crown of gold on his head
and a sharp sickle in his hand.
Then another angel . . .
cried out in a loud voice . . . ,
"Use your sickle . . . .
because the time has come."

REVELATION 14:1, 3–4, 6–7, 14–15

With these three images,
the *conflict* visions begin to fade.
It is time
to reward the faithful and
to punish the unfaithful.

The curtain falls on "Act 2"
as seven angels step on stage.
They hold seven bowls
filled with the anger of God.

The *judgment* visions are at hand.

What are my thoughts
as I imagine myself to be John
and ponder what all of this
should be saying to me?

"Act 3" (judgment visions) opens with
the seven angels pouring out the bowls
of God's anger on the earth (REVELATION 16:1–2).
The first five trigger a series of plagues.

Next the sixth bowl is poured. John says:

I saw three unclean spirits . . .
go out to all the kings of the world,
to bring them together for the battle
on the great Day of Almighty God . . .
in the place that in Hebrew
is called Armageddon.

Then the seventh angel poured out
his bowl in the air. A loud voice came
from the throne in the temple, saying,
"It is done!" . . .

Then [John] saw heaven open,
and there was a white horse.
Its rider is called Faithful and True;
it is with justice that he judges. . . .
The armies of heaven followed him. . . .
[He bears the name]
"King of kings and Lord of lords."
                REVELATION 16:13–14, 16–17; 19:11, 14, 16

Then they engage the armies of earth.
The battle is swift and decisive.
The dragon—"the Devil, or Satan"—
is chained a "thousand years."

(This symbolic time designates the era of the reign of Jesus' church on earth from the end of the Roman persecution to the Last Judgment.)

At the end of this era, Satan is freed and leads a final assault against the just. It ends with Satan and the army being "thrown into the lake of fire." John concludes:

I saw a great white throne
and the one who sits on it. . . .
All were judged. . . .
Those who did not have their name
written in the book of the living
were thrown into the lake of fire.
Then the one who sits on the throne said,
"And now I make all things new! . . .
I am the first and the last,
the beginning and the end. . . .
I am coming soon!"
REVELATION 20:11, 13, 15; 21:5–6; 22:7

The curtain falls on "Act 3" with John praying, "Come, Lord Jesus!"

What are my thoughts
as I imagine myself to be John
and listen to and record
these final words of the angel?

Three different interpretations
of the Book of Revelation have emerged
over the centuries.
We may call them:

- the early-history approach,
- the sweep-of-history approach, and
- the end-of-history approach.

The *early-history* approach
regards the book's primary audience
to be persecuted Christians
of the first century.
To these Christians the book says,
"Persevere and remain faithful
in your time of suffering!
Christ has conquered; so will you!"

The *sweep-of-history* approach
regards the book's primary audience
to be Christians of all times.
To these Christians it says,
"There will be times
of testing and suffering, but persevere;
the re-creation of the world
will take place according to God's plan."

Finally, the *end-of-history* approach
regards the primary audience
to be Christians who will be living
when the world ends. To them it says:

"Then the Son of Man will appear,
coming in a cloud
with great power and glory.
When these things begin to happen,
stand up and raise your heads,
because your salvation is near."
LUKE 21:27–28

Each of these three approaches
has profound merit and value.

The first approach makes Revelation
a guide for Christians of *early times*.
The second approach makes it
a guide for Christians of *all times*.
The third approach makes it
a guide for Christians of the *end times*.

Perhaps the best approach is to realize
that the Book of Revelation,
as the inspired word of God,
has a message for every Christian—
regardless of time or place.

"The few little years we spend
on earth are only the first scene
in a Divine Drama
that extends into eternity." EDWIN MARKHAM
What message does Revelation
hold for me personally right now?

343

James Cone's *God of the Oppressed*
describes the Sunday worship service
of black people in early America.

On Sunday morning,
after spending six days of struggling
to create meaning out of life,
the people . . . would go to church,
because they believed
that Jesus was going to be there. . . .
Sister Ora Wallace would line out
a familiar hymn. . . . The entire
congregation would join her . . . because
they felt the presence of Jesus. . . .

When the pastor would say,
"I know the Lord is in this place!
Can I get a witness?" the people
responded with shouts of praise,
saying "Amen" and "Hallelujah."

Through song, prayer, and sermon
the community affirmed Jesus' presence
and their willingness to try to make it
through their troubled situation.
Some would smile and others would cry.
Another person, depending upon
the Spirit's effect . . . would clap. . . .

All of these expressions were nothing
but black people bearing witness

to Jesus' presence among them.
He was the divine power in their lives. . . .

How could black slaves
know that they were human beings
when they were treated like cattle?
How could they know
that they were somebody
when everything in their environment
said that they were nobody? . . .
Only because they knew
that Christ was present with them
and that his presence included
the divine promise to come again
and to take them to the New Jerusalem.

The situation of these black slaves
parallels the situation of the seven churches
in the Book of Revelation.
They are able to carry on because
they believe Jesus is present with them
and will eventually lead them
into the glorious New Jerusalem.

"Come, Lord Jesus!"

To what extent is the situation
of modern Christians approaching,
slowly but surely, the same situation
as that of the early Christians?

1 WORLD OF OLD TESTAMENT

2 WORLD OF ABRAHAM

3 WORLD OF ISRAELITES

4 WORLD OF DAVID

5 WORLD OF PROPHETS

6 WORLD OF JESUS

7 WORLD OF PENTECOST

8 WORLD OF PAUL

9 WORLD OF EARLY CHURCH

Weekly Meeting Format

CALL TO PRAYER

> *The leader begins each weekly meeting*
> *by having someone light a candle*
> *and then reading the following prayerfully:*

Jesus said,
"I am the light of the world. . . .
Whoever follows me
will have the light of life
and will never walk in darkness."

JOHN 8:12

Lord Jesus, you also said
that where two or three
come together in your name,
you are there with them.
The light of this candle
symbolizes your presence among us.

And, Lord Jesus,
where you are,
there, too,
are the Father and the Holy Spirit.
So we begin our meeting
in the presence and the name
of the Father,
the Son,
and the Holy Spirit.